CONTENTS

W9-BXP-507

If, after reading through this book, you come up with an original D'var Torah that you would like to share with us...or, if you would like to share your answers to the "Food For Thought" questions...or, if you want to read some interesting answers to the "Food For Thought" questions — contact Gedalia at the Pitspopany Press e-mail: pop@netvision.net.il

HOW TO USE THIS BOOK

Over a period of one year the entire Five Books of the Torah are read in the synagogue. This book is divided into these weekly Torah readings.

In order to familiarize the reader with the Hebrew words and terms used when discussing the Torah readings, we have inserted Hebrew words in transliteration whenever possible. Instead of using the English phrase "weekly reading," we use the Hebrew word Parsha; and instead of calling our forefathers Abraham, Isaac, and Jacob, we call them by their Hebrew names, Avraham, Yitzhak, and Yaacov.

Of course, there are different ways to transliterate Hebrew. We decided that in most cases, the guttural *het* sound, as in *Hanukkah,* would be written with an *h*, rather than a *ch*.

Each chapter in the book covers one Parsha that is read during the week. However, during leap years, more than one Parsha is read on the same Shabbat.

Every Parsha has multiple sections that include:

This is a summary of the weekly Torah reading. The summary is textual, without interpretation. However, when translating from one language to another, sometimes the translation itself can end up being an interpretation. So I tried to find the most logical and understandable translation of words and phrases. When the Torah passages seemed ambiguous, I followed the interpretation of the great Sage, Rashi.

WISDOM
OF THE
SAGES
In this section you can find some short pearls of wisdom that have been passed down from generation to generation.

One of the main sources used in this section is the Midrash, a sort of storehouse of Rabbinic stories and interpretations that gives the reader greater insight into what is happening in the Parsha.

TELL IT
FROM THE
TORAH

Va'yikra ◆ B'midbar ◆ Devarim

Volume II

Written and Compiled by Gedalia Peterseil
Project Editor: Rabbi Yaacov Peterseil

PITSPOPANY

NEW YORK ◆ JERUSALEM

Dear Andrew,
You won't be here for us to give you a bar mitzvah gift, so we're getting you one early.
Mazel Tov —

Published by Pitspopany Press

Text copyright © 1998 Gedalia Peterseil

Design by Benjie Herskowitz

PITSPOPANY PRESS books may be purchased for educational or special sales by contacting: Marketing Director, Pitspopany Press, 40 East 78th Street, Suite 16D, New York, New York, 10021.
Fax: (212) 472-6253.

ISBN: 0-943706-97-1 (Cloth)
ISBN: 0-943706-84-X (Softcover)

Printed in Hungary

TABLE TALK
DVAR TORAH

This is the main d'var Torah. Its purpose is to develop a theme from the Parsha that anyone can repeat at the Shabbat table. Of course, you may want to add your own ideas or rework ours to fit your audience.

GEMMATRIA The word gemmatria comes from the Greek *geometria*, which means "calculations and measurements." Gemmatria sometimes gets a bit convoluted, but I've tried to make it as easy to understand as possible.

There are many different types of gemmatria. In the most commonly used form, each word in the Hebrew alphabet is given its own numeric value. By combining the numeric value of the letters in different words or phrases, hidden meanings can be found.

Here is a listing of the numeric value of each Hebrew letter.

Aleph = 1	Zayin = 7	Mem = 40	Koof = 100
Bet = 2	Het = 8	Nun = 50	Resh = 200
Gimmel = 3	Tet = 9	Sameh = 60	Shin = 300
Dalet = 4	Yud = 10	Ayin = 70	Taf = 400
He' = 5	Kaf = 20	Pe' = 80	
Vav = 6	Lamed = 30	Tzade' = 90	

FOOD FOR THOUGHT It is important to keep an open mind and question everything we read in order to get a better understanding of it. In this section I suggest a few of the more basic questions found in the Parsha which you may want to think about. Take this opportunity to think of questions yourself.

TELL IT WITH A SMILE The Talmud Shabbat (30b) tells us that the great Sage, Rabbah, would start his lectures with a joke. Rabbah realized that humor is an important vessel with which to clear the mind, enabling one to concentrate and understand better.

We tried to find humor that would relate to the Parsha. See if you can find the connection.

THE HAFTARAH CONNECTION

The source for reading the Haftarah comes from the Talmud Megilah (21a) which says that after reading the weekly portion, we must read a portion from the Prophets which is somehow connected to the Parsha.

There are a number of reasons given for this:

1) The commentator, Livush, says that King Antiohus of Greece prohibited the reading of the Torah in public. The Sages decreed that instead of reading from the Torah, the people should read from the Prophets. Every Parsha was given a Haftarah that would remind listeners what the Parsha was about. Even after the decree was abolished, the custom of reading the Haftarah continued.

The word Haftarah, according to some sources, comes from the Hebrew word *patur*, which means "exempt." Since there was a time when the Haftarah was read instead of the Parsha, the Haftarah was considered to exempt the listener from the Torah reading.

2) In ancient times it was the custom for everyone to stay in synagogue and study the Prophets after daily prayers. Later on, this custom disappeared because people had to hurry off to work. In modern times, the custom was reinstated on Shabbat, when one is prohibited from working.

This helps us understand another definition of the word Haftarah — "after." The Haftarah comes *after* the Torah reading. It signifies the end of the morning prayers.

Acknowledgments

First and foremost I want to thank God for watching over me when I needed Him most!

I want to thank my parents. There is no one in the world with whom I'd rather work than my father, someone whom I greatly admire and am very close with.

I wish to thank my siblings: Tehila, Shlomo, Nachum, Tiferet, Temima, Yosef, Todahya, and Tanya; and my brother-in-law Nitay, for their wonderful support and words of encouragement.

A special thanks to the Production Director at Pitspopany Press, Chaim Mazo, who even with the birth of his son, managed the Herculean task of getting this book out on time, and to Laurie Grossman for doing a terrific job editing and proofreading.

Words cannot express my gratitude to Rabbi Macy Gordon, a talmid hacham and close friend, for his invaluable remarks and insights.

I can't take credit for writing this book alone. There were many people who helped, whether by submitting their Divray Torah, or helping me sort out a few of the more difficult jokes. Thank you Shani Taragin for making sure I received the material on time.

This book is literally a world wide effort to bring Torah to all Jewish homes. I am indebted to the following people whose material has found its way, in some form, into these pages:

Debbi Bienenfield – Miami Beach, Florida
Ilan Chasan – Port Elizabeth, South Africa
Dov Daniel – Efrat, Israel
Adina Dear – Brooklyn, New York
Elisha Dickman – Yerushalayim, Israel

Mishael Dickman – Yerushalayim, Israel
Rachel Elbaum – Baltimore, Maryland
David Fuchs – Hertzaliya, Israel
Reuven Gafni – Yerushalayim, Israel
Shira Graber – Silver Springs, Maryland
Devora Holder – Toronto, Canada
Zeev Jacobson – Alon Shvut, Israel
Nadav Kidron – Yerushalayim, Israel
Yoni Kristt – Alon Shvut, Israel
Adiel Levin – Alon Shvut, Israel
Naomi Libicki – Columbus, Ohio
Zeev Meyerson – Alon Shvut, Israel
Paul Newman – Capetown, South Africa
Shlomo Peterseil – Sha'alvim, Israel
Michal Porat – Yerushalayim, Israel
Chaim Rand – Yerushalayim, Israel
Avital Silber – Rochester, New York
Hillel Solow – Yerushalayim, Israel
Sharone Tayar – Ontario, Canada
Dvir Tchelet – Alon Shvut, Israel
Caryn and Eldad Zamir – Alon Shvut, Israel
Chaggai Zamir – Alon Shvut, Israel

May we all be worthy to enjoy the fruits of our labor.

THE BOOK OF
VA'YIKRA

THIS WEEK IN THE PARSHA

A simple, straightforward exposition
of the weekly reading.

TABLE TALK
DVAR TORAH

A brief, cogent talk about the
weekly reading that can be
repeated at the Shabbat table.

FOOD FOR THOUGHT

Questions and concepts for
you to think about.

GEMMATRIA

Discusses the numerical value
of words found in the Parsha.

WISDOM
OF THE
SAGES

Rabbinic pearls of wisdom.

THE HAFTARAH CONNECTION

Explains how the Haftarah
connects to the weekly Parsha.

TELL IT WITH A

SMILE

A short humorous anecdote
that relates to the Parsha.

ויקרא

THIS WEEK IN THE PARSHA

The *Olah* Sacrifice

God tells Moshe what a person who brings a sacrifice to God, must do.

The *Olah* sacrifice, called the "Burnt Offering," is brought from an unblemished, perfectly healthy animal, which may be either a male bull, goat, or sheep.

The procedure of the offering is as follows:

Smiha: *The owner of the animal leans his hands upon the head of the offering, and declares why he is bringing this sacrifice.*

Shehita: *The animal is ritually slaughtered.*

Zrika: *The blood of the animal is collected in a sacred vessel and sprinkled on the Altar.*

Hafshata: *The animal is then skinned.*

Nitoa: *The animal is cut up into sections.*

Meliha: *Salt is sprinkled heavily on all the sections.*

Hakrava: *The sections of the animal are brought up to the Altar and put onto the fire until they are burnt.*

If the Olah is a turtle-dove or young dove, it must undergo the following:

Melika: *The Kohen uses his thumbnail to cut the bird's throat.*

Meetzuy Ha'dam: *The blood of the bird is squeezed near the Altar.*

11

Meliha, Hakrava: *The head of the bird is salted and burnt on the Altar*
Hasarat Murah: *The inner organs, the crop, of the bird are removed and discarded.*
Shisua: *The rest of the bird is split apart, salted, and burnt on the Altar.*

The *Minha* Sacrifice

God tells Moshe the laws of the *Minha* sacrifice, called the "Meal Offering."

The ingredients used for the Meal Offering are finely ground flour, oil, and frankincense.

When these ingredients are brought to the Kohen, he does *Kmitza,* which means "a handful." The Kohen takes three fingers-full from the offering and burns it on the Altar. The Kohen keeps the rest for himself.

This sacrifice can be baked, fried, or deep-fried, depending on why it is brought. The offering of the first barley grain of the year, called the *Omer*, is the only offering that is toasted.

All offerings must be salted. None of the offerings can be brought of leavened bread or sweetened.

The *Shlamim* Sacrifice

God tells Moshe the laws of the *Shlamim* sacrifice, called the "Peace Offering." This offering is brought from cattle, sheep or goats. It must be unblemished, but may be either male or female. It follows a similar process to the Olah Offering . However, unlike the Olah, only certain parts of the animal are placed on the Altar. The rest is divided between the owner of the animal and the Kohen, to be eaten.

The *Hatat* Sacrifice

God tells Moshe the laws of the *Hatat* sacrifice, called the "Sin Offering." For the most part, this sacrifice is brought to atone for serious sins that are committed unintentionally.

The sacrificial process differs slightly, depending on who is bringing the offering: the High Priest, the entire community, the ruler, or the individual.

The *Oleh V'yored* Sacrifice

This offering is a Hatat sacrifice, but it is brought based on a sliding scale of individual wealth. If a person cannot afford to bring a sheep or goat, he may bring birds. If he is too poor to buy birds, he may bring a Meal Offering without oil or frankincense.

There are basically four categories of people who bring an *Oleh V'yored* sacrifice. They include:

1) A person who does not testify, but should have testified.
2) A person who makes something holy, impure.
3) A person who swears falsely.
4) A person who doesn't keep his oath.

The *Asham* Sacrifice

The *Asham* sacrifice, called the "Guilt Offering," undergoes a process similar to that of the Sin Offering. However, the Guilt Offering is brought primarily for the following sins:

1) Using sacred property without permission.
2) Uncertainty as to whether or not one committed a sin that warrants bringing a Hatat.
3) Swearing falsely concerning financial matters.

13

WISDOM OF THE SAGES

Va'yikra, **"And He called..."** (1:1)

Why is the last letter of the word *Va'yikra,* the alef, written smaller than the other letters?

The Ba'al Ha'turim says that the small alef symbolizes Moshe's humility. Even though God would always call to him, Moshe perceived himself as being very small.

Why is the "Olah" the first offering mentioned?

One of the reasons for bringing this offering is to atone for impure thoughts. Rabaynu Bahi'ay explains that since thought precedes actions, an offering brought because of a thought should be mentioned before an offering brought because of an action.

"And if he will bring a Peace Offering..." (3:1)

Why is this particular sacrifice called a "Peace Offering"?

This offering is one that is enjoyed by everyone: The inner organs of the animal are placed on the Altar for God, the breast and thigh go to the Kohen, and the one who brings the sacrifice gets the skin and the rest of the meat. Since everyone gets a portion, it brings peace.

GEMMATRIA

M'solta U'm'shamna, "From its fine flour and oil" (2:2):

When someone sins and brings a sacrifice, he is hoping that God will accept his offering in place of his soul.

The Meal Offering consists of fine flour and oil. The word *Shamna,* "its oil," has a numeric value of 395. This is the same value as the word *Neshama,* "soul."

From this we see that God considers the Meal Offering to be a sacrifice which redeems the soul.

TABLE TALK
DVAR TORAH

In the beginning of the Parsha, the sons of Aaron are commanded to kindle the fire on the Altar.

In practice, however, they weren't the ones who first kindled the fire on the Altar. In 9:24 we read that the first fire was actually lit by God.

Similarly, when the Temple was dedicated, a fire descended from heaven to light the Altar.

If God is going to light the fire on the Altar, when does He expect the sons of Aaron to fulfill the commandment He gave them?

Rashi quotes the Sifra, saying: "Even though the fire comes down from Heaven, it is, nonetheless, a mitzva to bring fire as well."

This teaches us a lot about what is expected of us.

The fire, coming down from heaven, was proof that God accepted and approved of the Sanctuary. One might think that the only thing expected of us would be to keep the fire burning; to make sure we don't lose our connection with God.

But this is not the case. There is a mitzva for us to bring our fire as well. This teaches us that we must add to the holiness and sanctity of the Temple. We must not be content with stoking God's fire. We must bring our own fire in order to actively participate in making the Sanctuary God's dwelling.

Rabbi Yitzhak of Vienna believed this message to be relevant not only in worship, prayer, and devotion, but in our day-to-day Torah studies as well.

We must hold the Torah — both the Written and Oral Law — in great esteem. Every word found in the Talmud should be treated as if it were holy fire descending from Heaven.

But that should by no means deter us from expressing our own thoughts and ideas. Although we bow our heads in awe before the greatness of our ancestors, accepting their authority, we must actively make our own contribution in this world, as well.

THE HAFTARAH CONNECTION

(Yeshayahu 43:21-44:23)

In this week's Parsha we learn about the different sacrifices we can bring to God.

In the Haftarah, Yeshayahu the prophet tells the people not to think that they can atone for their sins by mechanically bringing sacrifices. Their sacrifices must be accompanied by true repentance. Yeshayahu concludes by telling B'nai Yisrael that it is better to listen to God and avoid sinning, than to sin and bring a sacrificial offering.

FOOD FOR THOUGHT

1) Why did God first call to Moshe before speaking to him? Usually God just appears without warning.

2) The Hebrew word *korban*, "sacrifice," is derived from the root *karov*, "close."
What does this teach us about the purpose of the offerings?

3) Why is it that the Kohen Gadol's Sin Offering is similar to that of the congregation, while a prince's Sin Offering is similar to that of a common man? (Chapter 4)

 **TELL IT WITH A SMILE**

There is a special sacrifice that must be brought when a leader sins. Even great people have to know when to say "I don't know."

In a small European city, there was a non-Jew who was widely acknowledged as an expert on Bible and languages.

He called on a representative of the Jewish people to debate with him. "We will ask each other a phrase in any language" he said, "and the first to say 'I don't know' will be forced to publicly admit that the other's religion is superior."

The Jewish community had a hard time finding someone to agree to debate with the wise man, but finally a simple peasant came forward and agreed to represent the community.

The debate was arranged, and the peasant asked the first question. "What does *ani lo yodayah* mean?"

The non-Jew answered immediately, "I don't know!" But even as he uttered the words he realized he had been tricked. "I don't know" was the translation of these Hebrew words.

When the peasant returned home, a great celebration was held, and one of the guests asked him: "Where did you get the idea to ask such an ingenious question?"

The peasant answered: "When I was a little boy, someone asked the Rabbi, a great scholar, to explain the phrase *ani lo yodayah*. The Rabbi answered 'I don't know.'

"So I figured, if the Rabbi who was such a great scholar didn't know, then there was a good chance this man wouldn't know either!"

17

צו

The Kohen and the Olah Sacrifice

God tells Moshe to command Aaron and his sons about the laws of the *Olah* sacrifice, the Burnt Offering.

The Burnt Offering is burned on the Altar all night. The skin of the animal is given to the Kohen performing the sacrifice. The Kohen must make sure that the *Aish Tamid*, "the everlasting fire," burns all night.

The Kohen and the Minha Sacrifice

God tells Moshe to command Aaron and his sons about the *Minha* sacrifice, the Meal Offering.

The Meal Offering is brought before the Altar. The Kohen takes a three-fingers full of the flour, mixes it with oil, and burns it, together with the frankincense, on the Altar. The rest is eaten by the Kohen.

A special Meal Offering is brought by a novice Kohen on his first day of service. It is also brought daily by the *Kohen Gadol*. This offering is soaked in oil, and then completely burned.

The Kohen and the Hatat and Asham Sacrifices

The Hatat sacrifice, the Sin Offering, and the Asham sacrifice, the Guilt Offering are eaten by the Kohen in the courtyard of the Mishkan.

If the meat of the sacrifice touches an object, that object becomes holy. If the meat is cooked in a metal pot, the pot must be cleansed before re-use. If the meat is cooked in earthenware, the earthenware pot must be broken. If the blood of the sacrifice touches a garment, the garment must be washed in a holy place.

The Kohen and the Shlamim Sacrifice

When the Shlamim sacrifice, the Peace Offering is brought, the officiating Kohen receives two parts: the chest and the right thigh.

The laws of one type of Peace Offering — the Thanksgiving Offering — differ significantly from the other Peace Offerings. This offering is brought with forty loaves of bread including:

10 unleavened loaves of bread mixed with oil

10 unleavened wafers smeared with oil

10 unleavened loaves of cooked fine flour mixed with heated oil

10 leavened loaves of bread

One loaf of each type is eaten by the officiating Kohen. It must be eaten within one day and a night.

Pigul

If the person bringing the sacrifice has an improper intention with regard to the sacrifice, his offering is considered *pigul,* "rejected," and must be burned.

For example, a Peace Offering must be eaten within two days.

If the person offering the sacrifice had in mind to eat the sacrifice on the third day, the sacrifice is rejected — even though the third day has not yet arrived.

Karet

If a person eats part of a Peace Offering while he is impure, he will receive the punishment of *karet,* a form of divine punishment.

Eating the fat of domestic animals, or the blood of any animal or bird is forbidden and is punished by karet.

The Inauguration of Aaron and his Sons

God tells Moshe to inaugurate Aaron and his sons as Kohanim, in front of the whole nation.

Moshe bathes Aaron and his sons, and puts the Kohen Gadol garments on Aaron. He then anoints Aaron, the Tabernacle and its vessels with oil. Finally, Moshe dresses the sons of Aaron in their Kohen clothes.

Certain sacrifices are brought and part of the blood is daubed on Aaron and his sons.

Aaron and his sons then go to the *Ohel Moed,* "tent of meeting," where they reside for seven days, concluding the inaugural period.

THE HAFTARAH CONNECTION

(Yermeyahu 7:21-8:3 9:22,23)

Our Parsha deals with some of the different sacrifices B'nai Yisrael had to bring.

In the Haftarah, Yermeyahu lists all of B'nai Yisrael's sins during the Temple period. One of the sins mentioned is that instead of sacrificing animals in the Temple, B'nai Yisrael built altars to sacrifice their own children to heathen gods.

The Prophet tells them that God wants them to do kind and just deeds, instead of sinning and bringing sacrifices.

WISDOM OF THE SAGES

"Command Aaron..." (6:2)

Rashi says that, when the word "command" is used, the commandment must be done quickly. Why?

In Tractate Kidushin we learn: "He who is commanded and fulfills the commandment is greater than he who isn't commanded and fulfills the commandment." The reason for this is that when we are commanded to do something, our evil inclination gives us many good reasons why we shouldn't. If we aren't commanded to do it, then our evil inclination leaves us alone.

Therefore we must always be quick about performing a commandment, otherwise our evil inclination might get the better of us.

"His soul will be cut off (karet) from his people." (7:20)

What does being "cut off" mean?

Some commentaries say that the person who commits a sin which is punishable by karet will live to see his children die. Others believe that God will shorten the sinner's life, and that he will die by the age of 50.

Yet others, like the Ramban, believe that there are different levels of karet, some of which include the loss of a person's share in the Next World.

"Gather everyone to the entrance of the Tent of Meeting." (8:3)

There must have been several million people gathered at the entrance of the Ohel Moed. How could so many people fit into such a small place?

Since the nation was united, a miracle occurred and everyone felt he had enough space. This teaches us that when the nation is united, there is enough room for everyone.

1) Why must an earthenware vessel in which something holy has been cooked be broken, while a metal vessel only needs cleansing?

2) What reason could there be for Moshe to place some of the blood of the inauguration sacrifice on Aaron's right ear, the thumb of his right hand, and the big toe of his right foot?

3) Why does Aaron bring a Sin Offering before he is inaugurated?

TABLE TALK
DVAR TORAH

Our Parsha elaborates on the sacrifices already mentioned in last week's Parsha. There is, however, a new sacrifice that is mentioned — the Thanksgiving Offering. It is mentioned as a type of Peace Offering, a voluntary offering, and has two special features: Forty loaves are brought with it, and it must be eaten on the same day.

This is very unusual, since the time allotted for eating all the other Peace Offerings is two days. Only compulsory sacrifices are eaten in one day.

Does that make the Thanksgiving Offering a compulsory or volntary sacrifice?

We can better understand the nature of this sacrifice when we realize that in King David's Psalm of Thanksgiving (Psalm 116) the reader is told how to praise God for saving him. The final stage is a Thanksgiving Offering, performed publicly, as the psalmist repeatedly writes, "I will pay God my vows in front of the whole nation."

In this public feast the individual thanks God, telling all those present of the miracle that happened to him.

Perhaps now we can better understand why this voluntary sacrifice has a hint of compulsory sacrifice added to it. The whole purpose of this offering is to publicly exclaim God's greatness. That is why the offering, with all its 40 loaves, must be eaten in one day. This compulsory law forces the individual to find a way to eat these 40 loaves. He must make a feast and invite friends to partake in it. At the feast he gets the opportunity to publicly tell his story. The miracle ceases to be his own, but becomes widely-known, encouraging people in their belief. The whole community is united, in praise of God .

In this way, the offering serves a double purpose. To let everyone know that God is watching over us, and to unite the whole community.

TELL IT WITH A SMILE

Hilda was telling her friend how royally her husband treats her.

"He is so wonderful," she boasted. "You know, he actually treats me like a god."

"You don't say," exclaimed her friend, impressed. "How does he do that?"

"Well," Hilda explained "every morning, without fail, he brings me a burnt offering — my toast!"

GEMMATRIA

Va'tikahel Ha'ayda, "And the community gathered" (8:4):

When Moshe inaugurated the Kohanim he was told to gather the community. What makes up the community?

The word *Va'tikahel,* "and they gathered," has the numeric value of 541. The word Yisrael has the same value. The entire nation of B'nai Yisrael was gathered because God wanted the whole nation to see the sanctification. This was to ensure that the Kohanim's legitimacy would never be doubted.

שמיני

The Inauguration of the Kohanim

On the eighth and final day of the dedication of the Mishkan, the Kohanim are inaugurated.

Both Aaron and B'nai Yisrael bring sacrifices. Aaron brings a Sin Offering and a Burnt Offering. The people bring a Sin Offering, two Burnt Offerings, two Peace Offerings, and a Meal Offering.

Aaron offers all the sacrifices. Then he raises his hands towards the people and blesses them.

Moshe and Aaron go into the Ohel Moed. When they come out, they bless the people. Then God's presence appears and a fire descends from heaven burning up the parts of the sacrifices that are God's. The people begin singing and then bow down.

Aaron's Sons Die

Nadav and Avihu, two of Aaron's sons, decide to make their own contribution to the ceremony. Each takes a pan, puts incense on it and lights it, offering the fire to God. But they were not supposed to bring the lit incense. A fire from heaven strikes and consumes them, and they die.

Moshe tells Aaron, "This is what God told me, saying, 'By those who are close to Me will I be sanctified, and I will be honored in front of the nation.'"

Aaron is silent.

Moshe calls Mishael and Eltzafan, Aaron's cousins, to take out the bodies. Then Moshe commands Aaron and his two remaining sons, Elazar and Itamar, not to show any signs of mourning, since they are anointed with the consecrated oil.

The Prohibition of Alcohol

God commands Aaron to refrain from drinking wine, or any alcoholic beverage, before he enters the Mishkan. This prohibition applies to all Kohanim, on pain of death. After all, they must be able to differentiate between the sacred and the profane, and between the pure and impure. They are also in charge of teaching the people the Laws of the Torah.

Aaron Argues with Moshe

Moshe sees that Elazar and Itamar have burned the Sin Offering instead of eating it. "This sacrifice was given to you to atone for the sins of the people," Moshe tells them. "You should have eaten it as I commanded!"

Aaron intercedes and says that God would not expect him to eat of the sacrifice on the day he has lost his sons.

Moshe hears his brother, and agrees.

The Laws of Kosher Foods

God tells Moshe and Aaron which animals may be eaten and which may not.

An animal is kosher if it has completely split hooves and chews its cud. Examples of non-kosher animals are: The camel, rabbit, and hare, which chew their cud but do not have completely split hooves, and the pig, which has completely split hooves but does not chew its cud.

A fish is kosher if it has fins and scales. All other seafood is not kosher.

All birds are kosher, except 20 birds that are listed in the Torah as non-kosher.

All flying and crawling insects are non-kosher. Certain hopping insects, however, are permitted.

The Laws of Purity

A person who touches the carcass of a forbidden animal is impure and has to immerse himself in a mikva. He then becomes pure that evening. If a person carries the carcass, he must go to the mikva, and immerse his clothes as well.

There are eight small animals whose carcasses create impurity in people, clothes, and utensils. Once the people, clothes, and utensils are immersed in a mikva and evening has come, they are pure again.

However, if one of these animals comes into contact with the inside of an earthenware vessel, everything in the vessel is impure, and the vessel itself has to be broken.

A well or spring cannot become impure.

Insects are not kosher, and God warns that eating them will not only make a person impure but repulse his soul as well. God is holy and wants His people to be holy as well. That is why God took the Jewish people out of Egypt.

TABLE TALK
DVAR TORAH

When God's presence descended, and the fire from heaven lit the Altar to inaugurate the Mishkan, the Jewish people witnessed one of the greatest moments in our history. It was the moment of forgiveness for the sin of the Golden Calf, and we were now, once again, the light in God's eye.

But the joy that the whole nation felt at this occasion was diminished by the death of two future leaders of B'nai Yisrael, Nadav and Avihu. For some reason, the eldest sons of Aaron entered the Holy of Holies with their own fire. The result was catastrophic. The very fire that symbolized forgiveness and closeness to God, entered their bodies and consumed them.

What happened? How could such a tragedy occur on such a great day?

The Rabbis suggest a number of possible sins that Nadav and Avihu may have committed in order to receive such an awesome punishment.

Some Sages suggest that Nadav and Avihu drank wine as part of the celebration and entered the Holy of Holies drunk. Others believe they sinned by offering a sacrifice that God had not specifically requested. Some even say that everything they did was correct; their sin was in not conferring with their elders — Moshe and Aaron — before doing what they felt was right.

But the question remains: If Nadav and Avihu were so great, how could they commit a sin on this special day? How could they violate God's Torah on the day when He entered the Mishkan?

The answer lies in the greatness of the day and their desire to come closer to God. Nadav and Avihu thought that it wasn't enough just to sit back and watch God's presence descend. In their desire to become closer to God, they rushed into the Holy of Holies, anxious to please and greet the Almighty. They wanted to see the source of their existence.

But by doing this, they ignored one of God's primary laws: No man can see God and live.

Nadav and Avihu got what they wanted. They saw God face to face, but they gave up their lives in the process.

People very often "lead with their emotions," letting their feelings get the best of them. The story of Nadav and Avihu helps us understand that a person must accept the Torah, with all its laws and commandments, not only on an emotional plane, but on a practical, logical level as well.

The Torah tells us what is best for us. It tells us how to conduct our lives. It is not devoid of emotion, but it asks us to control our emotions and do the commandments with all our hearts *and* with all our minds.

THE HAFTARAH CONNECTION

(Shmuel II 6:1-7:17)

Our Parsha deals with the eighth day of the consecration of the Mishkan. With the ritual completed, B'nai Yisrael now have at least a temporary structure in which they can communicate directly with God.

In our Haftarah, King David returns the Ark to its rightful resting place in Jerusalem. This deed inaugurated the beginning of the Temple period.

WISDOM OF THE SAGES

"Sacrifice your offering...and atone for yourself and the nation." (9:7)

The Ibn Ezra explains that Aaron first had to atone for himself, and only then could he atone for others. One must be free from sin if he wishes to act on behalf of others. That's why on Yom Kippur, the Kohen Gadol first brought his own offering, then his family's offering, and only then did he bring the nation's offering.

"Moshe heard and approved." (10:20)

Most of the time, Moshe was the one who spoke, and Aaron was the one who listened. Now the roles were reversed: Aaron spoke, and Moshe listened.

The Torah lets us know that Moshe approved of the role reversal. He enjoyed listening to his brother.

Listening to others is just as good, and for some, even better than doing the talking.

"These are the animals that you are permitted to eat." (11:2)

The Talmud Hulin 29 explains that Moshe actually showed each animal to the people. He did not deal in abstracts or talk above their heads. Moshe demonstrated the rules and laws of the Torah, leaving no doubt in anyone's mind what he was talking about.

He was the ultimate educator.

1) After Aaron's children are consumed by fire, his reaction is one of total silence. Aaron doesn't say a word. Why do you think he dealt with the death of his sons in such a fashion?

2) Why is the pig considered the epitome of a non-kosher animal? Why is it any worse than the camel or the rabbit? After all, at least it fulfills the criteria of having split hooves.

3) After God lists the non-kosher animals, He says that we shouldn't make ourselves impure, because He is the God who took us out of Egypt. What is the connection between the two?

GEMMATRIA

Yayin.. al taysht, "Don't drink any wine" (10:9)

The Kohanim are warned against drinking wine before serving God. The Hebrew word for "wine," *yayin,* has the numeric value of 70. One of the dangers of wine is that when you pour it into your mouth, it loosens the tongue, and secrets begin to pour out. The Hebrew word for "secret" is *Sod,* which also has the numeric value of 70.

TELL IT WITH A SMILE

Mr. Himmle wanted a fancy Bar Mitzva for his son, so he decided to hire one of the greatest chefs in the world.

Since the chef wasn't Jewish, he asked the Rabbi to go over the dietary laws with the chef, so that the affair would be kosher.

At the affair, everything was going smoothly until the main course was served. All the guests were horrified to see that the scales hadn't been removed from the broiled fish.

Mr. Himmle went straight to the chef and demanded an explanation.

"But sir," began the chef, "I prepared it exactly as the Rabbi instructed. He told me that Jews are absolutely forbidden to eat any fish that doesn't have scales!"

תזריע

THIS WEEK IN THE PARSHA

A Woman After Childbirth

God tells Moshe that a woman who gives birth to a boy is impure for seven days. On the eighth day her son is to be circumcised. For an additional 33 days she cannot go into the Mishkan or touch anything holy.

When a woman gives birth to a girl, she is impure for 14 days and cannot go into the Mishkan or touch anything holy for 66 days.

After her period of impurity, whether she gave birth to a boy or girl, the woman must bring a Burnt Offering and a Sin Offering.

Tzara'at

God explains to Moshe and Aaron the laws of *tzara'at*. (This affliction has superficial similarities to the disease of leprosy.)

Some of these laws are as follows:

If a person has tzara'at on his skin he is to be brought to Aaron or to one of his sons. Depending on how the skin looks, Aaron will either declare him pure, impure, or put him in quarantine for seven days.

If after being in quarantine for seven days, the tzara'at remains the same color and does not spread, then the person must be quarantined another seven days. If the tzara'at has diminished, the Kohen will declare him pure and he must wash his clothes in a mikva.

But if the tzara'at has spread on the skin, he is impure.

If a person has white tzara'at all over his body, the Kohen will declare him pure. If some healthy skin appears on him, the Kohen will declare him impure.

A person who has tzara'at must tear his clothes, let his hair grow, cover his lips with his clothing, and warn others by saying, "Impure! Impure!" As long as he has tzara'at he must stay outside the camp of B'nai Yisrael.

The Kohen is also to look at tzara'at that affects clothing. If he finds what looks like tzara'at on the cloth, he must quarantine it for seven days. If, after seven days, the Kohen finds the tzara'at has spread, the garment must be burned.

THE HAFTARAH CONNECTION

(Melahim II 4:42-5:19)

Our Parsha talks about someone who is inflicted with tzara'at, how it is discovered and the purification process.

The Haftarah proceeds to tell us a story about Na'aman, a high-ranking officer in the army of Aram, who gets tzara'at, and how he is purified by Elisha the prophet.

The Haftarah ends with a declaration from this officer proclaiming that there is no one like the God of Israel, for only He was able to cure him of his disease.

TABLE TALK
DVAR TORAH

This week's Parsha deals extensively with the laws of a person who is inflicted with tzara'at. This disease is not to be taken lightly. It entails a great deal of pain and suffering. It is a way for God to tell us to take stock of ourselves.

There are different reasons given in the Talmud for receiving tzara'at. They include haughtiness and *loshon hara,* "speaking badly" about someone.

These two transgressions are also interrelated. The Torah teaches us that we should be humble and not let our egos get the best of us. When we talk badly about someone, it is often because we feel superior to the other person. We are making ourselves higher, more important, at the expense of another.

That helps us understand one of the types of tzara'at mentioned this week, the *s'ayt.*

The s'ayt is a white blotch, slightly raised. It indicates that the person regards his behavior as pure and faultless, above all others. This is a sure sign that he is suffering from the disease known as "I-am-wonderful-itis." What we call, haughtiness.

This type of tzara'at may start out on one part of the body, but the Torah warns us, "Beware!" It spreads very quickly to the rest of the body. It must be stopped and treated in its early stages. That's why the Kohen tells the person with s'ayt to go into solitary confinement, away from everyone. He is to think about what he has done in life; how he treats others, and what he says about those he calls "friends." He has seven days to think about it. In seven days God created the whole world, and in this time the person is to re-create his world, his spiritual world.

The Torah tells us to try to prevent haughtiness and lashon hara by treating it in its early stages. This isn't too hard if we concentrate on our own faults, instead of harping on the faults of others.

1) Why is the time span of impurity for a woman who gives birth to a girl double that of one who gives birth to a boy?

2) Why must a woman who just gave birth bring a Sin Offering?

3) Why is a man partially covered with tzara'at considered impure, while a man who is completely covered with tzara'at is declared pure?

WISDOM OF THE SAGES "And on the eighth day he shall be circumcised." (12:3)

The Midrash says that this shows us the importance of Shabbat. The reason the brit is done on the eighth day is to make sure that the baby has experienced the holiness of a complete Shabbat.

"And the hair has turned white." (13:3)

The hair turning white is a sign of impurity. Why? Usually white is perceived as the color of something pure, like the clothes the Kohen Gadol has to wear on Yom Kippur.

Tzara'at is a punishment for speaking evil about someone. When a person speaks badly about another, he causes him embarrassment. People who are embarrassed often turn white. Therefore, that same color makes the person who spoke evil impure, and causes him embarrassment by forcing him to leave the camp of B'nai Yisrael.

"He will sit alone outside the camp." (13:46)

The Tractate Nedarim states that a person with tzara'at is like someone who is dead. This is because a person with tzara'at is on his own. He is away from all others. Yet, like most people, this person craves companionship and the interaction of others. For him, being ostracized is the equivalent of death..

 **U'va'yom ha'shemini yimol bisar orlato,** "And on the eighth day circumcise his flesh." (12:3)

The numeric value of this phrase is 1,067.

The Torah says a boy must be circumcised eight days after he's born. But when on the eighth day? There are many mitzvot that one can only do up until a certain time during the day. Is there a time limit for circumcision on the eighth day?

The words "the whole day is kosher for circumcision" also has the numeric value of 1,067, indicating that there is no time limit during the eighth day.

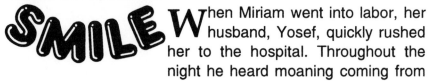

When Miriam went into labor, her husband, Yosef, quickly rushed her to the hospital. Throughout the night he heard moaning coming from her room. Soon he was a nervous wreck. He began to pace back and forth in the waiting room. The hours ticked by very slowly.

Finally, the doctor appeared and wished Yosef a hearty *Mazal Tov.*

"Is it a boy or a girl?" asked the anguished father.

"A girl," replied the doctor.

"Thank God," Yosef sighed. "At least she'll never have to go through what I just did."

מצורע

THIS WEEK IN THE PARSHA

Purifying the Metzora

God tells Moshe the process that will allow the *Metzora,* someone who has tzara'at, to re-enter the camp.

The Kohen goes to the metzora outside the camp of B'nai Yisrael. If he finds the metzora healed, the Kohen tells him to bring two birds. One bird is slaughtered, and its blood is caught in an earthenware bowl. The blood is sprinkled seven times on the metzora. The other bird is set free in a field.

The metzora washes his clothes, shaves all his hair, and im merses himself in a mikva. Then he can come into the camp, but he has to live outside his tent for seven days.

On the eighth day, the metzora brings a Guilt Offering, a Sin Offering, a Burnt Offering, and a Meal Offering.

House Tzara'at

God tells Moshe and Aaron that when B'nai Yisrael enter the Land, even houses may get tzara'at.

If a man thinks his house has tzara'at, he must go to the Kohen who will tell him to clear out his house. The Kohen will then enter the house. If he finds tzara'at on the walls, he must quar antine the house for seven days.

If the Kohen finds that the tzara'at spread, he must have the stones that are infected removed from the house, and all the mortar near the stones sent outside the camp. New stones and mortar are to be substituted for what was removed.

If the tzara'at returns, the house is demolished, and all the stones and mortar are taken outside the camp.

If the tzara'at has disappeared, the Kohen takes two birds and performs the same service he performs on a person who is cured, except that he sprinkles the blood of the slaughtered bird on the house seven times.

Zav

A man is a *zav* when he has certain sexual diseases. He is impure and anything he sits on is also impure. Another person touching his chair or bedding has to wash his clothes and himself in a mikva and wait until evening to be pure. Pottery that comes into contact with a zav has to be broken. Wooden utensils are to be rinsed in water.

When the man recovers, he must count seven days, and wash his clothes and himself in a mikva. Then he becomes pure. On the eighth day, he brings two birds to the Kohen. The Kohen takes one as a Sin Offering and the other as a Burnt Offering.

Niddah and Zavah

A woman in her menstrual cycle is called a *niddah*. Such a woman is impure for seven days. Anyone who touches her is impure until the evening. Another person touching her chair or bedding has to wash his clothes and himself in a mikva and wait until evening to be pure. If she has sexual relations during this time, the man becomes impure for seven days as well.

A woman is a *zavah* when she menstruates longer than is

normal for her or at an unusual time in her cycle. Her laws are similar to the laws of niddah.

THE HAFTARAH CONNECTION

(Melahim II 7:3-20)

Our Parsha deals primarily with the different types of tzara'at. As part of the purification process, the metzora must stay outside the camp.

The opening words of our Haftarah are "And there were four people who had tzara'at..." We read of how they entered the camp of the sworn enemy of the Jewish nation, Aram, and saw that the camp was deserted. Instead of just taking all the valuables they could find, they reported back to the king of Israel and succeeded in helping the Jewish nation in its time of distress.

FOOD FOR THOUGHT

1) **Why is the waiting period for a metzora seven days?**

2) **When the Kohen purifies the metzora, he dips his own hand into the blood of the slaughtered animal and then places some of it on the metzora's right ear lobe, right thumb, and right big toe. Why these three places?**

3) **Why should the owner of a house feel responsible if his house contracts tzara'at?**

TABLE TALK
DVAR TORAH

Our Parsha begins by describing the purification process that must be undergone by someone who has tzara'at.

The Torah states that the person who is cured of tzara'at must bring two live kosher birds, a piece of cedar, some crimson wool, and a hyssop branch.

Why these particular items?

Our Rabbis teach us that since tzara'at is brought about by the sin of haughtiness, the items brought relate to this sin.

The cedar is brought because it is a big tree which grows to tremendous heights. This represents the haughtiness of the person bringing it. The crimson wool and the hyssop branch are considered very lowly and show the person that in order to attain forgiveness he must try to become like them, humble and modest.

But where do the birds fit in? And why is one bird killed while the other is given its freedom?

Perhaps it is to tell us something about the other main reason that tzara'at afflicts a person: For the sin of *loshon hara*, speaking evil about someone.

The two chattering birds symbolize the gossip and slander that the person with tzara'at spoke.

The Kohen slaughters one of the birds and pours out its blood into a vessel. This is done in order to accentuate the redness of the blood and the fact that, by speaking evil, a person causes pain and suffering to another. Hopefully, the person will make up his mind to stop talking in ways that can hurt others.

However, one of the dangers of delivering this kind of message in such a powerful way is that the person who sinned might go to the other extreme. In his desire not to talk loshon hara ever again, he may decide to become a hermit and avoid contact with society. That's why the second bird is set free — to fly among the other birds. To show the person that life must go on, and that control, not withdrawal, is what God demands.

That is the lesson for all of us. To find the proper balance between watching what we say and functioning as useful, active members of society.

WISDOM OF THE SAGES

"He shall shave off all his hair — his head, his beard, and his eyebrows." (14:9)

The three places the hair is shaved off is to atone, in part, for three of the reasons that a person receives tzara'at.

The first reason is arrogance. This describes someone who feels that he is the best, above everyone else. That's why the head is shaven.

The second reason is loshon hara. He uses his mouth to speak evil. That is why the hair surrounding the mouth is shaven.

The third reason is the person's inability to see any good in people. That is why the hair surrounding his eyes — his eyebrows — are shaven.

"I have seen something like a disease on my house." (14:35)

When someone is sure that he sees a disease on his house, why does he tell the Kohen that he has seen something "like" a disease?

We're afraid that if he tells the Kohen that he definitely sees tzara'at, the Kohen will be influenced by him and fail to come to the correct conclusion.

From here we see how easy it is to be influenced by others, and how careful we must be.

"This is the Torah for all afflictions..." (14:54)

The Talmud Eyruvin 54a says that the remedy for a headache is to learn Torah. Similarly, the remedy for any part of the body that's aching is to learn Torah.

This is hinted at in our verse: "This is the Torah for all afflictions." If there is anything wrong with you, if you have any afflictions, then "This is the Torah" — the Torah is the remedy.

GEMMATRIA V'rahatz ba'mayim, "And he shall wash in water." (15:10)

Someone who has a disease of Zav must immerse in water in order to purify himself. How much water must he immerse in? Is it enough to take a bath or shower?

The word *ba'mayim*, "in water," has the numeric value of 92. This is the same numeric value as the words "in the waters of 40." This refers to the customary immersion in a *mikva*, which contains at least 40 se'ah (a liquid measurement) of water.

From here we learn that a mikva is the body of water in which the Zav must immerse himself.

TELL IT WITH A *Not everyone who peels his walls,*
SMILE *throws the paint away.*

Ralph went to visit his friend Danny, famed for being the town's biggest cheapskate. Ralph was very surprised to see his good friend scraping the paint off his walls and putting it in a suitcase.

"Danny!" exclaimed Ralph, "Are you redecorating?"

"No," answered Danny. "We're moving!"

אחרי מות

The Kohen on Yom Kippur

After the death of the two sons of Aaron, God tells Moshe to instruct Aaron about the Yom Kippur service.

Aaron is to work on Yom Kippur wearing four white garments. He is to bring a bull as a Sin Offering and a ram as a Burnt Offering. He must also take two male goats and one ram from the people; the goats are for a Sin Offering and the ram for a Burnt Offering. These offerings atone for his sins, his family's sins, and the sins of the entire nation.

The Two Goats

Aaron is to take the two goats and bring them to the entrance of the Ohel Moed. There, he draws lots. On one is written, "For God" and on the other is written, "For Azazel." The Goat that is for God is to be sacrificed as a Sin Offering. The other goat provides atonement for the people and is sent with a designated man into the desert to die.

The Holy of Holies

After he slaughters his Sin Offering, Aaron is to take hot coals from the Altar along with incense, and go into the Holy of

Holies. He is to place the incense on the hot coals so that a cloud of incense covers the Ark. He must be careful to do this so he does not die.

The Laws of Yom Kippur

On the 10th of the Jewish month of *Tishray,* a person must afflict himself by fasting, and not do any work. He must seek atonement and purify himself of his sins.

Yom Kippur is a special Shabbat and must be obeyed as a decree, forever.

Sacrifices in the Mishkan

God tells Moshe to tell Aaron, his sons, and all of Israel that sacrifices are to be brought only to the Mishkan. No one is to sacrifice to other gods, no matter how much they would like too. This is an eternal decree.

Covering the Blood

Anyone from B'nai Yisrael who drinks blood will be punished by God. Drinking blood is a sin because the life of the animal is in the blood, and blood is used during the sacrifices to atone for the lives of the people.

If someone traps an animal or a bird that is kosher, he has to pour the blood onto the ground and cover it. This is because the life is in the blood.

Nevayla and Terayfa

An animal that dies a natural death, or one that dies because it was hunted down, should not be eaten.

Forbidden Relationships

God tells Moshe that B'nai Yisrael are forbidden to do the things the Egyptians did, or the things the people who now live in Canaan do. B'nai Yisrael must observe the decrees and laws of God, and live by these laws.

Then God lists the forbidden relationships within the family unit, as well as the immoral relationships between male and male, and man and animal.

The Land of Israel is Holy

God warns the people that if they do any of these abominations, the Land of Israel will throw them out, because the Land does not want impurity on it.

1) How can the Kohen Gadol atone for the sins of the whole nation? Isn't everyone responsible for their own sins?

2) Based on what it says in our Parsha about blood, why does a child who hits his parents and draws blood receive the death penalty?

3) The Torah says that if we become impure in the Land of Israel, then the Land will regurgitate us. What does this tell us about the supposedly inanimate Holy Land?

47

TABLE TALK
DVAR TORAH

Following the tragic death of the two sons of Aaron, God appeared to Moshe and told him to tell Aaron not to enter the Sanctuary. The reason given is "because I (God) appear in a cloud on the Ark covering."

Rashi explains that since God is found there, Aaron shouldn't enter.

But doesn't it make sense for Aaron to go where God usually appears? He is the representative of the people to God. Where else should he go?

The answer lies in the well-known adage, "familiarity breeds contempt." While contempt is too harsh a word for what might happen if Aaron were to go into the Sanctuary whenever he wished, it is clear that familiarity often does diminish the awesomeness we feel about things.

If Aaron could enter the Sanctuary whenever he wished, it would begin to lose some of its grandeur. The spiritual experience that Aaron felt when entering the presence of God would inevitably diminish.

We see this effect of familiarity not only in the realm of our spiritual life, but in our everyday life as well. How many of us have little-used video games lying around? The same games that seem so enticing when first played have lost their shine. After a few weeks or months we become bored with them.

That's why Aaron could only enter the Holy of Holies once a year, on Yom Kippur, so that the full impact of what was happening would overpower him.

The Torah tells us that we have to treat our lives with that same awe. Our Sages say, "Everyday the commandments should seem new to you." We have the power to make the commandments feel new. We have the power to create "new-ness" in what we learn and what we do. We must use our intel-lect and imagination to overcome the pitfalls of familiarity and bring excitement and freshness into everything we do.

WISDOM OF THE SAGES

Before the Kohen Gadol enters the Holy of Holies on Yom Kippur, why does he change from his special golden garments to the white garments worn by regular Kohanim?

Our sages say that "A prosecutor cannot become a de-fender."

The golden garments serve as a prosecutor against the peo-ple because they remind God of the sin of the Golden Calf. Therefore, the Kohen Gadol can't ask God to forgive B'nai Yis-rael on Yom Kippur while wearing golden garments.

Part of the Yom Kippur service was selecting lots. This lot-tery decided which of the two goats would be thrown off a cliff and which would be sacrificed to God. Throwing the goat over a cliff was a symbolic act meant to rid B'nai Yisrael of their sins. The sins were placed on the goat's head, making it the very first "scapegoat" ever!

"And you will keep my commandments...and live by them." (18:5)

From the words "and live by them," we learn that — with the exception of murder, adultery, and idolatry — danger to one's life overrides all the commandments in the Torah, including Shabbat. These words show us that God would rather that we live to fulfill the commandments than die trying to fulfill them.

49

GEMMATRIA

B'zot yavo Aaron, "With this will Aaron come..."(16:3)

The verse uses the word *B'zot,* "with this," to tell us how the Kohen Gadol is supposed to approach the Sanctuary of God. Its numeric value is 410. For 410 years the Kohen Gadol served in the Sanctuary of God, until the First Temple was destroyed.

THE HAFTARAH CONNECTION

(Yehezkel 22:1-19)

Our Parsha deals with the Yom Kippur service and explains how it helps to purify the people. The rest of the Parsha reveals what must be done to keep holiness within the nation.

In our Haftarah we read that the Kingdom of Yehuda has sunk to a very low level of morality. The people are told that they will be thrown out of the Land, because they did exactly the opposite of what God commanded.

TELL IT WITH A SMILE

Two poor Jews were discussing the wonderful lives led by the rich and famous.

"Did you know that Yankel the baker puts on a clean white shirt every Shabbat?" asked Talman.

"That's nothing," replied Yenta. "Feivel the jeweler puts on a clean white shirt twice a week!"

"Well, how about Aaron, the Kohen Gadol," Talman said, not

willing to be outdone. "Didn't he change shirts five times during Yom Kippur?"

Yenta thought for a moment, and then smiled. "Perhaps so. But I have heard that Baron Rothschild, with all his wealth, puts on a new shirt and then takes it off, on the hour.

"It's a wonder he has any time to make money!"

קדושים

THIS WEEK IN THE PARSHA

Keeping Holy

God commands Moshe to tell B'nai Yisrael, "You shall be holy for I, your God, am holy."

God then details a series of commandments that will help B'nai Yisrael attain their goal of holiness. These commandments include:

Revering parents.

Observing the Shabbat.

The prohibition of turning to idols.

Leaving gleanings of the field for the poor.

The command to "love your neighbor as yourself."

The prohibitions of stealing, lying, swearing falsely, cursing the deaf, placing a stumbling block in front of the blind, and favoring the poor or honoring the great in judgement.

The prohibitions against superstition, sorcery, idol worship, cutting yourself as a sign of mourning, giving one's children as a sacrifice to the Molech god, and making a tatoo.

The prohibitions of gossiping, hating another Jew in

your heart, taking revenge, and bearing a grudge.

The prohibition against using a razor to completely shave off the hair of your sideburns and your beard.

The prohibitions against immoral behavior.

Forbidden mixtures

This includes the prohibition of mating two animals of different species, planting your field with mixed seeds, and wearing a garment made of two fibers, wool and linen.

Orla

Orla is the law that prohibits a Jew from eating the fruits of a tree during its first three years of growth. In the fourth year, the fruit is sanctified to God, and in the fifth year it may be eaten by everyone.

Respect for the Elderly

A person must rise for an old man, and honor the presence of a Sage.

Weights and measures

Scales, weights, and measures of all types must be correct.

Forbidden Relationships

The Torah lists the forbidden sexual relationships within the family unit, as well as those within Jewish society. It also specifies the punishments for these relationships.

Keeping Kosher

B'nai Yisrael must distinguish between pure and impure animals, as God had already commanded them. In this way the people will be holy.

Holiness is the reason God has separated B'nai Yisrael from the other nations.

WISDOM OF THE SAGES

"Don't place a stumbling block in front of a blind person." (19:14)

Although the verse can be understood literally, our Sages tell us that it comes to teach us an important lesson. Each and every one of us has a "blind spot" somewhere. We must not take advantage of each other's weaknesses, but rather help one another overcome them.

"You shall not take revenge..." (19:18)

Why isn't one allowed to take revenge?

If a man bites his lip by mistake, does he then go and bash his teeth in? Similarly, B'nai Yisrael are all one entity. When you hit someone else, it is as if you are causing damage to yourself.

"Love your neighbor as you love yourself." (19:18)

In this week's Parsha we read the well-known words, "Love your neighbor as you love yourself." Rabbi Akiva said that this is a great rule in the Torah.

The corollary to this rule was voiced by the great Sage, Hillel. A man once came up to him and asked to be taught the entire Torah while standing on one foot.

Hillel replied, "What you would hate someone to do to you, don't do unto others." That is the basis of the whole Torah.

THE HAFTARAH CONNECTION

(Amos 9:7-15)

Our Parsha describes at length how Jews must maintain a high moral standard. Proper behavior is rewarded, while improper behavior is punished.

The Haftarah tells us of a day that God will inflict punishment upon those of B'nai Yisrael who sin. But God promises that He will not destroy the house of Jacob.

God tells us that He will punish those that don't behave correctly. Yet, despite the destruction, there will be rebirth.

GEMMATRIA

V'lo tash'hit, "And you shall not destroy" (19:27)

The Torah forbids us to destroy our beards. What does "to destroy our beards" mean?

The numeric value of the phrase equals 1,155. The phrase "this is with a blade not a scissors," has the same numeric value. We can see from here that while it is prohibited to use a razor to shave the beard, it is permissible to use scissors.

TABLE TALK
DVAR TORAH

This week's Parsha begins with the commandment for all of B'nai Yisrael to be holy.

Rashi explains that this holiness is actually a prerequisite for fulfilling most of the commandments in the Torah. That's why it had to be said in front of the whole nation.

Right after this commandment, the Torah proceeds to give a list of different mitzvot that must be observed. If we look carefully at the different mitzvot, we find that they fall under two separate categories: Commandments between man and God, such as keeping the laws of Shabbat, and commandments between man and man, such as not coveting your neighbor's possessions .

The Ateret Mordehai explains that many people incorrectly assume that holiness only applies to the relationship between man and God. We reason that since God is holy, all our dealings with Him must be conducted in holiness as well.

However, when it comes to commandments between man and man, we tend to think that holiness isn't necessary. People are only people and get what they deserve.

The Torah comes to teach us that that is precisely why we are all commanded to be holy. If everyone maintains a holy level in their lives, then everyone must treat his neighbor as someone holy. If that is the case, then how can one holy person even think of stealing, hurting, or mistreating another?

It is this holiness that separates us from other nations, and crowns us as God's chosen nation.

1) Why is it that when it comes to fearing parents, the Torah mentions the mother before the father (19:3). However, when it comes to honoring parents, it is the father who is mentioned first (Shemot 20:12)?

2) Throughout the Parsha, there are certain commandments that end with the words, "I am the Lord, your God." Is this phrase placed randomly, or is there a common denominator among these commandments?

3) Where, in our Parsha, is there a source for "the Good Samaritan law"?

Joel and Paul were walking through a zoo. Suddenly they saw everyone turn and run towards them. They stopped someone and asked her what the commotion was all about.

"Didn't you hear?" she panted, "One of the lions in the zoo has escaped and is coming this way. You better save yourselves!"

Hearing this, Joel immediately took out his sneakers and put them on.

"Are you crazy?" asked Paul. "Even with those running shoes you'll never be able to outrun the lion."

"I don't have to outrun the lion," replied Joel. "I just have to outrun you!"

אמור

The Laws of a Kohen

God tells Moshe to instruct the children of Aaron about the laws of a Kohen. These laws include the prohibition of coming into contact with a corpse unless it's an immediate relative: wife, mother, father, son, daughter, brother, or unmarried sister.

Kohanim are also prohibited from pulling out their hair, shaving their beards, or deliberately cutting themselves as signs of mourning.

They cannot marry a woman from any of these three categories: a *zona,* a divorced woman, or a woman born from a relationship forbidden to a Kohen.

The reason for all these prohibitions is that the Kohen is holy to God.

The Laws of a Kohen Gadol

The *Kohen Gadol* is not allowed to become impure for anyone, even for his deceased parents.

He must not let his hair grow long or tear his clothes as a sign of mourning.

A Kohen Gadol may only marry a virgin.

Blemishes on a Kohen

God tells Moshe that there are certain blemishes that disqualify a Kohen from serving in the Mishkan.

Some of the blemishes mentioned are blindness, lameness, and a broken arm or leg.

Although having a blemish prohibits the Kohen from serving in the Mishkan, he is still allowed to eat the sacrificial food.

Keeping the Sanctity of the Offerings

God tells Moshe to explain to Aaron and his sons that a Kohen who is impure isn't allowed to bring or eat an offering.

He must first purify himself by immersing himself in a mikva, and waiting until nightfall.

Eating the Teruma

A Kohen may only eat his teruma, if he is pure.

Any slave of the Kohen may eat from the teruma.

A Kohen's daughter who marries a non-Kohen is no longer allowed to eat teruma. However, if she is widowed or divorced, and has no children, then she may once again eat teruma when she returns to her father's house.

A non-Kohen who eats teruma in error must return an equal amount of food, plus an additional one-fifth, to the Kohen.

Animals with a Blemish

God tells Moshe to inform Aaron and his sons that no blemished animal will be accepted as an offering.

Some of the blemishes are blindness, broken limbs, or growths.

Laws for the Offerings

God tells Moshe that a newborn ox, sheep, or goat must be with its mother for seven days before being eligible as a sacrifice. Furthermore, an ox, sheep, or goat can't be slaughtered with its offspring on the same day.

The Thanksgiving Offering should be brought to gain God's favor, and must be eaten by the following morning.

Shabbat and Festivals

God tells Moshe to speak to B'nai Yisrael about Shabbat and the Festivals.

Work may be done during the six days of the week, but the seventh day must be one of complete rest, a holy day in which no work may be done.

Passover is a seven day holiday, beginning on the 15th of the first month, *Nissan*. During that time, no leavened bread may be eaten.

When B'nai Yisrael enter the Land, they must bring an Omer (a certain measure of ground barley) from the harvest to the Kohen. The Kohen waves the Omer before God and brings other sacrifices as well. This occurs on the second day of Passover.

Starting the second day of Passover, the people must count 50 days. The 50th day is Shavuot, and the First Offerings of new grain are brought.

On the first day of the seventh month, *Tishray,* no work may be done. It is a holy day in which the *Shofar* is sounded as a remembrance.

The 10th day of the seventh month is a day of atonement. It is called Yom Kippur. No work may be done. Everyone must fast. Anyone who doesn't afflict his soul will receive the punishment of karet.

The seven day holiday beginning on the 15th day of the seventh month is called Sukkot. During Sukkot, B'nai Yisrael must live in a Sukka (hut). This commemorates the fact that when B'nai Yisrael left Egypt, God gave them huts to dwell in. They also have to hold the *arba minim,* "four species."

The Ner Tamid

God tells Moshe to command B'nai Yisrael to take pure olive oil and light the *Ner Tamid,* "the perpetual lamp," in the Ohel Moed. Every evening Aaron is to prepare the lamp so it can be lit the next morning.

The Showbread

Twelve loaves of bread must be baked every week, and arranged before God on Shabbat. Aaron and his children must eat this bread in a holy place.

The Death of the Blasphemer

Shlomit, the daughter of Divri from the tribe of Dan, has a son by an Egyptian man. This son fights with another Israelite and curses, using God's name. He is brought before Moshe and placed under guard. Moshe awaits God's verdict.

God tells Moshe that a blasphemer, someone who curses using God's name, must be stoned to death.

A Man Who Injures

A man who kills another man shall die.

A man who inflicts a wound on his friend has to pay full damages.

A man who kills an animal must pay the owner its worth.

THE HAFTARAH CONNECTION

(Yehezkel 44:15-31)

Our Parsha talks about the different laws that the Kohanim must keep. The purpose of these laws is to make sure that they stay pure and holy, so they can point B'nai Yisrael in the right direction.

In our Haftarah, the prophet Yehezkel reveals God's words to the Kohanim who followed in His path. The prophet repeats the laws pertaining to the Kohanim that are written in our Parsha. This is done so that they will know what is expected of them and fulfill their obligations accordingly.

TABLE TALK
DVAR TORAH

At the end of this week's Parsha we come across a most unusual and unpleasant story.

Two people, one of whom is described as "an Israelite man," and the other "the son of an Israelite woman," get into a fight in the middle of the camp. During the fight, the son of the Israelite woman blasphemes God's name and pronounces a curse. As a result, he is brought to Moshe, who then places him in jail. Moshe asks God what to do. God tells him that the blasphemer is to be killed by stoning!

What drove this man to curse God's name? How could he curse the God who had just taken him out of Egypt and performed all those miracles for him?

The Torah states that he was the son of an Egyptian man and an Israelite woman. According to Jewish law, he was considered a Jew. However, he was a Jew without a tribe. Since a person's tribe, and therefore his right to inherit, is derived from his father, this person had no land to call his own.

The Midrash tells us that, since his mother was from the Tribe of Dan, the man had automatically assumed that this tribe would take him under their wing, and provide him with a piece of land.

It is not hard to imagine how hurt this man was when he realized he had no future among the tribes. Worse still, when he argues with the tribal representative, the man is taken to court where Moshe rules against him.

It was at this point that the man stormed angrily out of the court and into the camp, blaspheming God.

According to this Midrash, the blame for this terrible sin was not entirely his own. Those who brought him to court, and those who refused to help him, were partially to blame for his predicament. They should have offered him some way to save face; some way to feel like a brother among the people. But he was left to his own devices, and ultimately, died because of them.

This may explain why all of B'nai Yisrael had to be present at the stoning. They were forced to confront the fact that they had all been at least partially responsible for this man's death.

That is a lesson for all of us. We must be careful not to belittle those whom society treats as outcasts. We should not push them away, causing them to sink to even greater depths. When someone calls out for help, we must, all of us, answer.

1) Why can't a Kohen with a blemish serve in the Temple?

2) Are the Festivals that are mentioned in the Parsha, written in a specific order, or just inserted at random?

3) Can you find the verse in our Parsha that is customarily recited over wine during the festivals? Why was this verse chosen?

GEMMATRIA

V'hu isha vivtuleha..., "and he shall take a maiden..." (21:13)

The numeric value of the word *v'hu*, "and he" is 18. This teaches us that a boy should get married when he's 18 years old!

This is reinforced by Yehuda ben Tayma who writes in Pirkay Avot (5:25): "An 18 year old goes to the canopy."

WISDOM OF THE SAGES

"On the eve of the ninth day of the month..." (23:32)

This verse tells us that we should fast on the ninth of Tishray. But doesn't Yom Kippur fall out on the 10th day of Tishray, as it says earlier in 23:27?

The Talmud Brahot 8b points out that from this verse we learn that anyone who eats a lot on the ninth and then fasts on the 10th, is considered by God as if he fasted on the ninth and the 10th.

There were some sages who walked around all day with a candy in their mouth in order to fulfill this Mitzva to its fullest!

"And on the first day you should take for yourself." (23:40)

From this verse the Sages learn that the *arba minim*, the "four species," are *Etrog, Lulav, Hadasim, Aravot*.

"An eye for an eye." (24:20)

The Talmud states that this verse is obviously not to be taken literally, but rather, refers to a monetary payment.

If that's correct, why didn't the Torah just state that if someone knocks out an eye, he has to pay the equivalent of his eye?

Rav Soloveitchik believes that if the Torah would have talked about money, people wouldn't understand the severity of maiming a person. It would cause them to be indifferent to the suffering of others because they would automatically be thinking of what the wound was worth in dollars and cents.

TELL IT WITH A SMILE

Moti Silverberg, a well known professor at Cambridge University, is notified that the Queen has decided that he is to join the elite group of people about to be knighted.

Right before the ceremony, all the knights-to-be are briefed. They are each given a line in Latin that they must recite.

When Moti approaches the Queen, he's so nervous that he forgets his lines. He quickly comes up with the only non-English verse that he knows: "Ma nishtana ha'lyla ha'ze mi'kol ha'laylot?" (Why is this night different from all other nights?)

To which the queen, in utter shock, turns to her aide and asks: "Why is this knight different from all other knights?"

בהר

Shmitta

On Mt. Sinai, God instructs Moshe to tell B'nai Yisrael about *Shmitta,* the seventh, or "Sabbatical" year.

When they enter the Land of Israel, B'nai Yisrael are allowed to plow the Land for six years, but in the seventh year they have to let the Land rest. They are forbidden to do any type of work on the Land, including sowing and harvesting, both in their fields and vineyards.

During the Shmitta year, B'nai Yisrael, their slaves, and their animals will be able to eat from whatever grows on their fields, but they may not sell their produce.

Yovel

From when they enter the Land, B'nai Yisrael should count seven straight Shmitta years — 49 years in all. The 50th year is the *Yovel,* the "Jubilee" year. During the Yovel, no work may be done on the Land.

This year is to be made holy to God by sounding the shofar on Yom Kippur.

Any Land that was sold during the course of the previous 49 years is to be returned to its original owner. Land can't be sold indefinitely because all Land belongs to God. Therefore, when Land is sold, the number of years until Yovel should be taken into account before settling on a price.

If B'nai Yisrael keep these laws, then the Land will give enough produce during the year prior to the Shmitta and Yovel to sustain the nation for three years.

Redeeming Property

If someone becomes poor and has to sell his land, a relative should redeem it — buy it back. If the poor person saves up enough money, he must buy the land.

If a man sells a residence in a walled city, he must redeem it within a year. If it isn't redeemed during that period, it belongs to the new owner even after the Jubilee.

However, the Levites homes can always be redeemed. If they are not redeemed, they return during the Jubilee. The reason for this is that these homes are their heritage.

Their fields cannot be sold because the Land is their eternal heritage.

Helping the Poor

If a fellow Jew has financial problems, you should strengthen him. Don't take any interest from him.

A Jewish Slave

If a Jew is sold to another Jew, it is forbidden to make him perform "slave labor."

During the Jubilee year, he and his family are set free. The reason for this is that God took B'nai Yisrael out of Egypt to be His slaves.

A non-Jewish slave is not set free during the Jubilee.

If a Jew is sold to a non-Jew in the Land of Israel, he must be redeemed by his relatives. In any event, the Yovel year redeems him, although the owner must be compensated for the loss.

Idolatry and Shabbat

It is forbidden to make idols or erect statues.

B'nai Yisrael must observe Shabbat and be in awe of the Mishkan.

THE HAFTARAH CONNECTION

(Yermeyahu 32:6-27)

Our Parsha deals with the laws pertaining to the Shmitta and Yovel years. One of the major laws regarding ownership of land is that it must be redeemed if sold to another person.

In our Haftarah, God tells Yermeyahu to redeem his cousin's land. This redemption comes at a time when B'nai Yisrael are on the verge of being destroyed by their enemies. In redeeming his cousin's land, Yermeyahu shows B'nai Yisrael that they must have faith that God will save them from their enemies.

 If you ever forget how many years the Yovel cycle is, there is an easy way to remember it. The word *B'yovel*, "In a jubilee (year)," has the numeric value of 50. Yovel comes around once every 50 years.

TABLE TALK
DVAR TORAH

Our Parsha deals primarily with Shmitta and Yovel, the cycles of 7 and 50 years that the Land of Israel must rest. But inserted within the Parsha are a number of other laws, including laws about slavery, idol-worshipping, and Shabbat. Why do these laws follow the laws of Shmitta and Yovel?

The idea behind the Shmitta year is very similar to the concept of Shabbat.

Just as God created the world in six days and rested on the seventh, so too man must work for six days and rest on the seventh. On Shabbat, we have the time we need to fully appreciate the world we live in. We have the perfect opportunity to remember and acknowledge that God created the world, and continues to sustain it.

During the Shmitta year, we also acknowledge that the earth belongs to God, since He was the one who created it. We realize that we are but "hired hands" on His earth. We have His permission to eat from the produce, but we must remember: "The whole Land belongs to Me (God)." (25:23)

Yovel comes along after seven complete Shmitta cycles. In this 50th year, not only is all farming forbidden, but any Land that was sold is returned to its original owner. This serves as a reminder to us that though property can be sold and bought, we don't really own it at all.

Jewish slaves are also set free during the Jubilee. This brings home the fact that we can't own a fellow Jew. We are all servants of God, His "property." Therefore, we shouldn't be slaves to others.

Finally, one who worships idols rebels against the idea that there is one sovereign God who rules over the entire world. For him, there is a god of the sun, another of the moon, and yet another presiding over each of the stars. Every one of these gods has their own domain. It's a pantheon of gods that don't have the time to deal with men, usually because they are at war with each other.

So we see that all the commandments in the Parsha revolve around the same concept: God's insistence that the Jewish people recognize the fact that the world and its inhabitants belong to God. And that all we have is given to us, on loan, from God's storehouse of riches.

FOOD FOR THOUGHT

1) Find at least two significant differences between Shmitta and Yovel.

2) The Torah forbids one to lend a fellow Jew money and charge interest. How then can we explain the dealings of a Jewish bank which lends money and charges interest?

3) Our Parsha talks primarily about the different laws of Shmitta, Yovel, and other commandments as they apply between man and man. How do the last two verses in the Parsha, dealing with the prohibition of making idols, fit in?

WISDOM OF THE SAGES

"And you shall not deceive your fellow man." (25:17)

There are those who take this verse one step further. Not only don't they deceive their fellow man, they also don't deceive themselves. As Shakespeare said, "This above all, to thine own self be true..." If you're honest with yourself, you'll be honest with others.

71

"If your brother falls...you should support him." (25:35)

Why are the verses prior to this one written in the plural, while this one is in the singular?

Sometimes, when someone needs help, we volunteer others to help him, saying that they are closer relatives or wealthier friends.

That's why the Torah specifically uses the singular. You are to look at this unfortunate fellow as though you are his only brother, and therefore, the only one around to help him.

"You shall not take any interest from him." (25:36)

Why is it prohibited to lend money to a fellow Jew and charge interest?

Rabbi Zalman Sorotzkin explains that the most important thing we have in life is "time." Time is what puts everything into perspective. In truth, we should be sad at every passing moment, for each one brings us closer to "the day of reckoning."

But someone who lends money and charges interest has the exact opposite feeling. Every second that passes brings him great joy, because he is making more interest on his money.

 *During the Yovel, land goes back to its original owner, even if the person who bought it loses money. Here's a novel way of redeeming moveable property.*

A man went into a department store and ordered a shirt. The clerk wrapped up the package and gave it to him.

"I'm sorry," said the customer, "I've changed my mind. I would like to exchange this for a pair of pants instead."

"All right," replied the clerk.

The customer selected the pants, and when the clerk had wrapped the purchase and handed it to him, the man started to leave.

"Hey, you forgot to pay for that," shouted the clerk.

"What are you talking about?" the customer called back. "I just traded in the shirt for them."

"Yes, but you didn't pay for the shirt either," said the clerk.

"Why should I?" came the smug response. "Did I keep it?"

בחוקתי

THIS WEEK IN THE PARSHA

The Blessings and Curses

God tells B'nai Yisrael that if they walk in God's path and keep His commandments, then He will bless them.

These blessings include a prosperous year in which the Land gives good produce, B'nai Yisrael triumph over all their enemies, and God bring peace to the Land.

God will place his Mishkan in the nation, walk among them, and make them His people.

However, if B'nai Yisrael don't listen to God, then He will bring punishments upon them. God lists 49 punishments He will bring, including:

Physical punishments such as swelling and high fever, as well as attacks by enemies.

Agricultural punishments such as drought and famine.

Nature-oriented punishments such as plagues of wild animals.

Punishments that will bring disease and hunger, and lead to the destruction of the cities of B'nai Yisrael and the exile of the people from their Land.

But God promises that even when B'nai Yisrael are in exile, He won't forget His covenant with their forefathers, and will not destroy them completely.

Evaluating Gifts to the Temple

God tells Moshe that if a man vows to bring the value of a person as a present to the Mishkan, he must follow a formula that takes into consideration the person's gender and age.

Redeeming Animals Houses and Fields

When a man pledges his animal, house, or field to God it must be evaluated by the Kohen. The value is redeemed for money and given to the Kohen.

Ma'aser

A person who wants to redeem the *ma'aser,* the "tithe" he sets aside for God from his land, may do so by adding a fifth of the value of the ma'aser.

The proper method for evaluating ma'aser from cattle and sheep is to count the animals as they are herded into a pen. Every 10th one is to be set aside as ma'aser.

In many congregations it is customary to read the curses in the Parsha quickly and quietly. This is symbolic of our wish to do away with the curses and give them as little emphasis as possible.

"Five of you will chase 100, and 100 of you will chase 10,000." (26:8)

God tells B'nai Yisrael that they will destroy their enemies.

But the math doesn't make sense. If five chase 100, then 100 should only be able to chase 2,000, not 10,000?

This shows us how people can draw strength from each other. If there are five people, each one will only be able to chase 20. But if you have 100 working together and giving each other strength and support, then each person will be able to chase 100 people.

"These are the laws and the Torot that God gave to Moshe." (26:46)

The word *Torot*, the plural of the word Torah, is used here in order to let us know that there were two Torahs given to Moshe. One is the Written Torah, which everyone can read for him or herself. The other is the Oral Law which, although passed down from generation to generation, is no less important than the written one. Indeed, without the one, the other can't be understood.

THE HAFTARAH CONNECTION

(Yermeyahu 16:19-17:14)

In our Parsha, God tells us that if we follow in His path, He will bless us and the Land. If, however, we fail to do so, then we will be punished.

Our Haftarah emphasizes the reward for following in God's path by comparing man to a tree. If we put our faith in people, we will be like a tree in the desert, always wondering how it will get some water. However, if we put our faith in God, we will be like a tree by the river, never fearing where its water will come from, even during a drought.

TABLE TALK
DVAR TORAH

This week's Parsha begins on a very positive note. God tells the nation that if they follow His path and keep His commandments, then He will bestow many blessings upon them. These blessings include the assurance that God will walk among B'nai Yisrael and be their God, and they, in turn, will be His nation.

However, if they will not listen to God and keep His commandments and, instead, insist upon straying from the path of God, then He will punish the nation.

If we look closely, we can find a direct correlation between the blessings and punishments. We will either follow God and live in peace in a Land of milk and honey, or we will choose to ignore the path of God and live in fear in a barren Land.

Then, midway through the punishments, God tells the people, "And if (with all these punishments going on) you walk with Me casually, then I will increase the punishment of your sins seven-fold." (26:21)

What could the people do to get seven times more punishment? Are there worse sins than not walking in God's ways? Why is walking casually worse than walking arrogantly or not walking at all?

Rashi explains that the Hebrew word *Keri,* "casual" carries the implication of "by chance." This suggests that while all these curses are occurring, the people casually carry on with their lives, suffering and accepting their punishment. They see everything that is happening to them as a matter of chance, a coincidence. They don't relate to their troubles as a warning by God; God doesn't even come into the picture. They are casual about the whole thing.

"Things are terrible," they say, watching their crops whither and their livestock die, "but life is cyclical. It'll be better next year."

In Judaism, there is no coincidence. As long as you believe that God interacts in this world, there cannot be chance, because God controls the world.

So why are the people going to be punished with curses that are seven times worse than those already enumerated?

Because in not seeing the Hand of God in what is happening to them, B'nai Yisrael lose their chance to atone. And without atonement, and the realization that you have done something wrong, there is no hope for forgiveness and blessing.

That is why God points out, clearly, for all to see, that even if the punishments come, you can still eventually receive the blessings as long as you don't walk casually with God, and ignore His role in the world.

1) Why are there so few blessings compared to the amount of curses in our Parsha? What does this show us about the power of blessings?

2) At the end of the curses, God says that He will remember His covenant with Yaacov, Yitzhak, and Avraham. Since Avraham was our first forefather, shouldn't the order be reversed?

3) Why are there specific values for the worth of people? Why not leave it up to the courts to decide the value of someone based on his or her worth in the community?

GEMMATRIA

V'natati Mishkani b'tohahem, "And I will place My Sanctuary within you."(26:11)

The Hebrew word *Mishkan*, "Sanctuary," has the numeric value of 420. This represents the 420 years that the Second Temple existed.

TELL IT WITH A SMILE

The Council of Elders in Chelm were worried. They had no jail in Chelm. What if they caught a thief? What would they do with him?

Everyone volunteered an answer. But finally, the Rabbi came up with what seemed to be the best solution. "We'll drill two holes in the wall of the bath house. The prisoner will be forced to pass his hands through the holes, and will have to keep them there for as long as the judge decrees."

"I don't think that will work," protested one of the elders. "Suppose he simply withdraws his hands and walks away before completing his sentence?"

"That's no problem," replied the rabbi. "Once he passes his hands through the holes we'll order him to make a fist. That way he won't be able to withdraw his hands without unclenching them!"

THE BOOK OF
B'MIDBAR

THIS WEEK IN THE PARSHA

A simple, straightforward exposition of the weekly reading.

TABLE TALK
DVAR TORAH

A brief, cogent talk about the weekly reading that can be repeated at the Shabbat table.

FOOD FOR THOUGHT

Questions and concepts for you to think about.

GEMMATRIA

Discusses the numerical value of words found in the Parsha.

WISDOM OF THE SAGES

Rabbinic pearls of wisdom.

THE HAFTARAH CONNECTION

Explains how the Haftarah connects to the weekly Parsha.

TELL IT WITH A SMILE

A short humorous anecdote that relates to the Parsha.

במדבר

The Census

In the second month (Iyar) of the second year after the Exodus, God tells Moshe to take a census of B'nai Yisrael. He, Aaron, and a representative from each tribe, are to count every male from 20 years and over who would be eligible to go to war.

The total number counted is 603,550.

However, the Levites are not counted together with the rest of the people.

The Order of Travel

God gives Moshe and Aaron specific instructions on how to set up camp around the Mishkan.

To the east of the Mishkan the tribes of Yehudah, Yesahar, and Zevulun make camp. To the south of the Mishkan the tribes of Reuven, Shimon, and Gad camp. The Levites camp around the Mishkan. To the west of the Mishkan the tribes of Ephraim, Menashe, and Binyamin camp. And to the north of the Mishkan the tribes of Dan, Asher, and Naftali camp.

When the people travel, Yehudah's group goes first, followed by Reuven's group, then the Levites carry the Mishkan, after which Ephraim's group move out, and finally, Dan's group leaves.

The Census of the Levites

God tells Moshe that the Levites will be in charge of the Mishkan and it's vessels. Now, he is to count every male Levite from one month and above. There are three families within the Tribe of Levi: Gershon, Kehat, and Merari.

The total number of Levites is 22,000.

Redeeming the Firstborn

God tells Moshe to count every firstborn male from the Children of Israel from one month and above.

The total number of firstborn males is 22,273.

The Levites are to take the place of the firstborn of B'nai Yisrael. God explains that on the day that He struck down the firstborn of the Egyptians, the firstborn of B'nai Yisrael were sanctified to Him.

Each firstborn of B'nai Yisrael is to be redeemed with a Levite. The extra 273 firstborn are to be redeemed with five shekels. The redemption money is to be given to Aaron and his sons.

1) Why wasn't the Tribe of Levi counted along with the rest of the tribes?

2) Why were the Levites counted from the age of one month, and the rest of B'nai Yisrael from 20 years and above?

3) When B'nai Yisrael pitched camp, or were on the move, every tribe had a set place. Was it randomly chosen or is there a reason why each tribe was specifically put where it was?

TABLE TALK
DVAR TORAH

The book of B'midbar begins with Moshe and the rest of the heads of tribes counting B'nai Yisrael.

This "counting" reminds us of some of the other times B'nai Yisrael were counted in the desert. The first time we encounter it is after B'nai Yisrael sin with the Golden Calf. We see it again in the Parsha of Pinhas (which will be read in a few weeks time), where they are counted right after the plague.

In the Prophets we find it once more when King David decides to count the nation. But this time, because he counted the people, the entire nation is punished, and a plague kills many in the camp.

Why the discrepancy? Is counting the nation a positive thing or is it something negative?

Rashi, in our Parsha (1:1), says that God counts us many times in order to show His love for us. According to this, counting is definitely a positive thing.

The commentator known as the S'forno says that counting each person actually highlights their individuality. It shows that no two people are alike. Every one of us has their own job to do in life. All the individuals combined form a nation, where everyone uses their individual talents for the benefit of the whole.

However, there are also negative sides to the counting of B'nai Yisrael: First of all, B'nai Yisrael's strength is unlike the strength of other nations. The other nations' main strength is in their numbers. The greater their number, the greater their influence.

B'nai Yisrael, on the other hand, influence the world not because of their number, but because they are the only nation that fulfills God's commandments. It doesn't matter how many people there are in B'nai Yisrael, what matters is how they conduct themselves as a Jewish nation. Quality, not quantity is of the essence.

In addition, B'nai Yisrael are not supposed to act like a bunch of individuals thrown together, who's motto is: "Every man for himself." The uniqueness of the Jewish nation is in their togetherness, the fact that every Jew is responsible for his fellow Jew.

So, we see there is potential for positive and negative in the counting of B'nai Yisrael. That's why Moshe only counted the people when he received a direct order from God, as in this week's Parsha. In this way, he knows that the reasons for counting are good reasons, reasons of God.

King David, on the other hand, didn't get permission from God to count the nation. He had his own reasons, reasons that were clearly not in line with God's, and therefore a plague ensued.

We must learn from this that man cannot presume to second-guess God. Our job is to use our individuality for the benefit of B'nai Yisrael, so that as a nation we can fulfill our goal of being a holy people to God.

Toward this end, we can all count ourselves — in!

GEMMATRIA   **Saviv la'Mishkan,** "Surrounding the Mishkan (they shall dwell). (1:50)

The Kohanim and Levites were in charge of the work in the Mishkan. As a result, they were situated around the Mishkan, and had to be careful to maintain a very holy state. This can be seen by comparing the numeric value of *Saviv La'Mishkan* which is 514, to that of *Ahm Kadosh,* a holy nation, which is also 514.

WISDOM OF THE SAGES

"And God spoke to Moshe in the desert saying." (1:1)

The Midrash says that the Torah was given through three things: fire, water, and the desert. The fire and water symbolize two opposites, teaching us that the Torah is best learned with another friend who thinks in a different way than you do. The desert is symbolic of the humility that must be a part of our personality if we want to be able to keep the Torah.

"As they rest, so too shall they travel." (2:17)

There are people who keep all the commandments in the confines of their home. But when they go outside their homes and mix with other people, they conveniently *forget* what it means to be a representative of the Jewish people. In this sentence we are told that when we travel we should make sure to remain the same people that we are at home.

"And these are the offspring of Aaron and Moshe..." (3:1)

Why does the Torah treat Aaron's children as though they belonged to Moshe too?

The Tractate Sanhedrin (9b) states that Moshe used to teach Aaron's children Torah. From here we learn that whoever teaches his friend's children Torah, it is as if he brought them up!

THE HAFTARAH CONNECTION

(Hoshea 2:1-22)

Our Parsha deals primarily with the counting of B'nai Yisrael in the desert.

In the Haftarah, the prophet Hoshea speaks of the future redemption. He begins by stating that "B'nai Yisrael will be as numerous as the sand on the seashore, which is so plentiful it can't be measured."

Both the Torah and the Haftarah show us that numeric greatness is also a part of B'nai Yisrael's legacy.

TELL IT WITH A SMILE

Three Jews were driving through the desert, when all of a sudden their car died.

They knew that their only hope for survival was to reach civilization. Since they were in for a long walk, each person took the item he considered most valuable, with him.

The first one chose the water that was left.

"A wise choice," his friends told him.

The second took food so that they would have what to eat. "Good thinking," his friends commended him.

The last one went to the car, broke off the car door, and put it on his back.

"Why on earth do you want to take the car door for?" asked his astonished friends.

"It's really quite an important thing," he explained, "because this way, if we ever get too hot, we can always roll down the window and cool off!"

נשא

THIS WEEK IN THE PARSHA

Counting the Levites Who Work

God tells Moshe and Aaron to count the males in the Levite families who are between 30 and 50 years of age — the period of time when they may work in the Mishkan.

The total number of working Levites is 8,580.

Purity of the Camp

God tells Moshe to send out of the camp of B'nai Yisrael people infected with *tzara'at* or *zav*, and anyone who has come into contact with a human corpse. This is done so that they will not contaminate the place in which God's presence resides.

Stealing

God tells Moshe that a man or a woman who steals and denies it under oath, actually commits treachery against God. In order to be forgiven, the person who stole has to confess his sin and return what was stolen, plus an extra one-fifth of the item.

If the person robbed is a convert and dies, leaving no relatives, then the robber has to return payment to the Kohen, along with a sacrifice of atonement which the Kohen will sacrifice for him.

The Sota

God tells Moshe what to do if the wife of a man strays and she is seen to go willingly with another man into a secluded place. If there are no witnesses to testify what happened between them, and the husband is jealous — having previously warned his wife not to do such things — then he should take his wife to the Kohen. He must also bring with him an offering of barley flour, called a jealousy offering.

The Kohen brings her into the Mishkan. He takes sacred water in a clay vessel and adds earth from the floor of the Mishkan into the vessel. These are called the "bitter waters." He then uncovers the woman's hair and puts the jealousy offering into her hands.

The Kohen has the woman swear she will accept whatever happens to her. He tells her that if she has had intimate relations with someone other than her husband then she will be cursed: The bitter waters in the vessel will cause her thigh to collapse and her stomach to swell up.

She then answers "Amen! Amen!"

The Kohen writes the curse on a scroll and erases the letters in the bitter waters. He then gives her the bitter waters to drink.

Then the Kohen sacrifices the jealousy offering.

If she has been unfaithful to her husband the curse comes true. If she is innocent then she will bear a child.

The Nazir

God tells Moshe that a man or a woman who proclaims a Nazirite vow in order to be closer to God, must make sure that he:

1) Does not cut his hair.

2) Refrains from drinking wine or eating grapes.

3) Does not come near a human corpse.

If someone dies near the Nazir suddenly, without warning, then he must shave his head and bring certain sacrifices. The days he was a Nazir are forfeited.

But if nothing happens during this time and he concludes his Nazir time then he has to come to the Ohel Moed with both a Sin Offering and a Peace Offering to God. The Nazir must shave his head and then take his hair and put it on the fire which is under the Peace Offering. When the rituals have all been completed, the Nazir can drink wine and eat grapes.

The Blessings of the Kohanim

God tells Moshe that Aaron and his sons should bless the Children of Israel with three blessings:

May God bless you and safeguard you.

May God shine His face upon you and be gracious to you.

May God turn His face to you and establish peace for you.

The Princes of the Tribes

On the day that Moshe finally set up the Mishkan, the princes of Israel brought their offerings before God. This included six covered wagons and twelve oxen. Moshe gave the wagons and oxen to the Levite families, Gershon and Merari, to help them carry the items in the Mishkan that were their responsibility. But he didn't give anything to the family of Kehat since the items they had to carry had to be carried on their shoulders.

For the next 12 days, one prince each day brought his offerings. All the offerings were identical.

Moshe Enters the Mishkan

Moshe entered the Mishkan and heard the Voice speaking to him from the top of the Ark cover, from between the two Cherubim.

THE HAFTARAH CONNECTION

(Shoftim 13:2-25)

In our Parsha we read the laws of a Nazir.

In the Haftarah, we read the story of a Nazir called Shimshon (Samson). We see that when he keeps the Nazirite laws he is able to defeat all the nation's enemies, but when he breaks these laws, he succumbs to his enemies.

1) Why does the topic of Nazir come right after that of Sota? Are wine and immoral sin somehow connected?

2) When a Nazir finishes his Nazarite vow, he has to bring a sin offering. Why? Is taking the Nazirite vows somehow considered a sin?

3) At the end of the Parsha, the Torah tells us what each "prince" of tribe gave. Right after that, the Torah calculates how much was donated in total. Why must the Torah waste precious words? Couldn't we have done the math?

TABLE TALK
DVAR TORAH

At the end of our Parsha, the heads of the tribes each bring offerings to commemorate the consecration of the Sanctuary. Interestingly enough, all the offerings are exactly the same.

We know that the Torah is very careful not to insert any extra words. If that is true, then why didn't the Torah simply write at the end of the offerings of the first prince, "and the rest of the heads of the tribes gave exactly the same."

In two other places in the Torah, the same question arises. The first time is when Eliezer, Yitzhak's servant, is sent to find a wife for Yaacov. There the Torah tells us about the test that Eliezer prayed for to ensure that he found the right woman. Later on the Torah relates Eliezer's prayer and the realization of that prayer, almost word for word, when Eliezer meets Rivkah's brother.

The second time is with the building of the Mishkan. Initially, the Torah goes into all the details of what was to be created for the Mishkan, and then repeats everything again when the Mishkan is actually built.

Why is it that the Torah goes into such lengthy descriptions with regards to these three things?

Rabbi Zeharya Breuer says that these three things are the basic pillars of Judaism, and therefore merit such lengthy descriptions.

The choosing of a spouse is the groundwork for building a family that will follow in God's path, and therefore Eliezer's experience is mentioned twice.

The Mishkan is the sanctuary in which we serve God. The Torah wants us to participate in the joy and happiness accompanying every stage of the creation of a home for God's spirit, from the planning stage all the way to the actual building of the Mishkan.

The Torah also wants each and every tribe to be proud of it's prince when he brought his offerings. Every member was supposed to feel as if he was actually accompanying his representative during this holy task.

We see that there are three different spheres that make up the essence of our community. The first is the family unit, the second is religion, and the third is our nationality. All three things play a vital role in making us who we are.

WISDOM OF THE SAGES

Why were the Kohanim chosen to be the ones to bless the people?

Rabbi Aaron Volkin explains that the success of a blessing is based on the sincerity of the one giving the blessing. Since the sole income of the Kohanim was derived from the terumah that B'nai Yisrael gave them, and the terumah depended on a successful harvest, you could always be sure that the Kohanim meant every word of their blessing.

"And He will bring you peace." (6:26)

The Tractate Brachot (56b) says: "If you dream of a pot, expect peace."

What's the connection between a pot and peace?

Reb Tzvi explains that there's nothing like a pot when it comes to making peace. A pot takes two extremes, water and fire, and enables them to come together. That's what peace is about!

The sacrifice for the first day was brought by Nahshon. Why

is he the only head of a tribe who's title, "Nasi," is not added after his name?

A title only has to be used in cases where it adds honor to a name. In Nahshon's case, however, no title was necessary to give him honor. His fame preceded him. The Midrash tells us that the when B'nai Yisrael left Egypt and were stopped at the Red Sea, it was Nahshon who had the guts to walk into the sea. When the waters reached his neck, they split. Since that event, everyone knew who Nahshon was. He alone didn't need the title, "Nasi".

GEMMATRIA There are 15 words in *Birkat Kohanim*, the blessings of the Kohanim. The last word in these blessings, *Shalom*, which means "peace", "hello", or "goodbye", comes after 14 words. Fourteen is equivalent to the numerical value of the word *Yad*, hand. That is why it is customary when greeting someone, to shake his hand (Yad) and then say, "Shalom."

TELL IT WITH A SMILE

At the end of the Parsha, the Torah adds up the total contribution that each prince brought to the Mishkan. For some people, adding numbers is a lot more complex then it appears.

There is a story told of a diner who walked into the tavern in the city of Chelm. When he finished his meal he asked the owner for the bill. She told him that the steak was seven kopeks, and the spare ribs another seven, altogether eleven kopeks.

"Madam," the honest man informed his host, "seven and seven is fourteen, not eleven."

Rather than thank him for correcting her error, the woman insisted her math was correct.

"Years ago my husband died and left me with four children," she explained. "I married my second husband who also had four children. We then had another three children together. Now, he has seven children, and I have seven children, yet together we have eleven. Two times seven are clearly eleven!" she insisted.

Unable to find a flaw in this logic, the man paid up and left.

Lighting the Menorah

Aaron is told to light the Menorah. The three wicks on the right and three wicks on the left of the Menorah are all to be directed toward the middle lamp.

The entire Menorah is made of one piece of solid gold.

Purifying the Levites

God tells Moshe to purify the Levites. He is to sprinkle water of purification on them. They are to shave their entire bodies, and immerse their garments.

The Levites are to take two young bulls for sacrifices. Moshe is to take the Levites to the Ohel Moed where all the people are to meet. There, the Children of Israel will lean their hands on the Levites. Aaron will lift each Levite. Then the Levites will lean their hands on the oxen. Then Moshe is to lift each Levite. The Levites are to be separated from the people and lifted once more in front of the Ohel Moed.

After this, the Levites begin to work in the Ohel Moed.

Purpose of the Levites

The firstborn were saved by God in Egypt and belong to Him. But God decided to substitute the Levites for the first born. The Levites are to work for the Children of Israel and provide atonement for them in the Ohel Moed. In this way no one impure will work in the Ohel Moed and there will be no plague among the people when they approach the holy places in the Ohel Moed.

The Levites are to work full time from 30 to 50 years of age. From age 25 to 30 they are to apprentice as Levites.

The Second Pesach

In the second year of the Exodus from Egypt, God tells Moshe that the people are to make a Pesach sacrifice on the fourteenth day of Nisan, in the evening.

But there are those who have been in contact with a human corpse and therefore impure. They can't make the sacrifice. Yet, they want to be part of the Pesach sacrifice as well.

God says that anyone who is impure, or anyone too far away to come back for Pesach can make the Pesach sacrifice on the fourteenth of the following month, in the evening. But, at the same time, God warns the people that anyone who can make the Pesach sacrifice, and doesn't, will receive karet.

Silver Trumpets

Moshe is told by God to make two silver trumpets. The different blasts on the trumpets will indicate when the camp is to move, assemble, go to war, celebrate holy days, etc. The Kohanim are to blow the trumpets.

The Order of Travel

B'nai Yisrael travel in the desert as follows:

First the Tribe of **Yehuda** breaks camp, followed by the Tribes of **Yisahar** and **Zevulun**.

Then the Mishkan is taken down by two of the families of Levites, **Gershon** and **Merari**.

The Tribe of **Reuven** rises, followed by the Tribes of **Shimon** and **Gad**.

The third family of Levites, **Kehat**, then carry the Mishkan.

The Tribe of **Ephraim** breaks camp, followed by the Tribes of **Menashe** and **Binyamin**.

Finally, the Tribe of **Dan** begin to leave, and the Tribes of **Asher** and **Naftali** follow.

Moshe Asks Yitro to Join Them

Moshe asks his father-in-law, Reuel, who is also called Yitro, to join them on their journey to Israel. But he refuses to go with them. Moshe pleads with Yitro, promising that God will take good care of him.

The Aron on the Journey

When the Aron begins to travel through the desert, Moshe says, "Arise, God, and Your enemies will be scattered, and those who hate You will run from You."

When the Aron rests, Moshe says, "Return God, to the many thousands of the Children of Israel."

Tired of the Mahn (Manna)

The people begin to complain, and God sends a fire that burns the edges of the camp. Moshe prays for the fire to stop, and it does.

Again some of the people complain. This time they say, "Who will feed us meat? We remember the free fish we ate in Egypt." They tell Moshe how tired they are of the mahn.

The mahn, however, is pleasing to look at and easy to find. People can cook it in many ways and it tastes like dough kneaded with oil. At night, the dew comes down and the mahn falls on top of it.

Moshe Complains

Moshe becomes frustrated at the constant complaints of the people. He says to God, "Did I give birth to these people that I have to take care of them like a nursemaid takes care of an infant? Where am I going to get meat for all of them? It's just too much! If this is how You treat me, then kill me God!"

The Seventy Wise Men

God commands Moshe to gather 70 wise men who will be known as the "elders of the people." He is to bring them to the Ohel Moed. There, God will take some of the spirit that is in Moshe and place it on them. In this way, Moshe will not have to take care of the people alone.

Moshe does as God asks. When some of the spirit that was in Moshe rests on the 70, they begin to prophesy.

Eldad and Medad

Two men continue to prophesy long after the others have stopped. Eldad and Medad run through the camp prophesying. Yehoshua, the servant of Moshe, wants them put in jail. But Moshe says, "I wish all the people could be prophets."

Quail

God sends a wind to bring in quail from the sea. The quail are everywhere, piled high all around the camp. When the people get up in the morning, they begin to collect the quail. They collect piles of quail all day and the next day.

But, while they are still eating the quail, God sends a plague among the people, and those that complained die.

Speaking Evil About Moshe

Miriam and Aaron discuss Moshe's family life, and speak about his Cushite wife. They are upset and say, "Did God just speak to Moshe? He speaks to us as well." God hears this and is angry. After all, Moshe is the most humble person in the world.

Suddenly, God confronts Moshe, Aaron, and Miriam, telling them to go to the Ohel Moed. He calls to Aaron and Miriam and tells them that while they hear God through dreams, God speaks to Moshe, "mouth to mouth," in a clear vision.

"Why did you not fear to speak against My servant Moshe?" God says, accusingly.

God's spirit leaves the Ohel Moed and Miriam is covered with a white disease called tzara'at.

Moshe begs God to heal his sister. But God tells him, if her father were angry with her, wouldn't she hide her face from him? So too, she must spend time out of the camp.

Miriam goes outside the camp for seven days. The people wait for her before proceeding onward.

1) Who is given the opportunity to make a second Pesah? Why did they deserve such an opportunity?

2) Why did the nation complain about the manna? Do you think they really had better food in Egypt?

3) How can we learn from this week's Parsha that tzara'at comes as a punishment for speaking badly about someone?

THE HAFTARAH CONNECTION

(Zeharia 2:14-4:7)

Our Parsha begins with a description of how the Menorah should be lit.

In the Haftarah, the prophet Hoshea describes a vision he has of the Menorah. An angel tells him that this is symbolic of the fact that victory against our enemies will be achieved not with might, nor with force, but with the spirit of God.

TABLE TALK
DVAR TORAH

Our Parsha states that "The man Moshe was very humble, more so than all the men on the face of the earth." (12:3)

Moshe, undoubtedly the greatest leader B'nai Yisrael ever had, and the only human being able to confront God at will, is clearly a figure that we have to try to emulate.

What exactly does the Torah mean when it says that Moshe was humble? Why is it so important, that our Sages singled out its opposite — arrogance — as the root of all character flaws?

The Torah says: "Love your neighbor as you love yourself." (Va'yikra 19:18) . In order to fulfill this mitzvah, it is obvious that one must first love himself! Yet how can we love ourselves without feeling arrogant and egocentric?

To understand what is needed of us, we should look at the moon. The moon, the greatest luminary we have at night, is only able to light our path because of the light it reflects from the sun.

So should the Jewish people feel before God. One shouldn't belittle himself and think that he is worthless. One should shine out just as the moon does at night. Yet, just like the moon, it is important to realize that our abilities and specialties — our light — is a reflection of a greater source. Whatever we have is given to us through God.

The feeling of dependance on God is a very uplifting one. A person who feels great because of his own powers, is limited to the extent of his own powers. However, one who recognizes that his gifts are from God, will never feel limited in his abilities.

Humility is the ability to love yourself but with the knowledge that your "self" is but the reflection of the greater "Self" of God.

WISDOM OF THE SAGES As compensation for not being able to participate in the bringing of the donations for the Mishkan, our Sages say that Aaron was given the job of lighting the Menorah.

The Midrash explains that Aaron received the better part of the deal since the offerings the Kohanim gave could only be brought as long as the Temple stood, while the lamps were to be kindled forever.

But if the Temple is destroyed then there is nowhere to light the Menorah either?

The Ramban explains that the Menorah discussed is not only the Menorah of the Sanctuary, but includes the Hanukkah Menorah we light each year.

In the Parsha, before and after the passage of *Va'yehi bin-soa ha'Aron...* "And when the Aron began to move" (10:35,36), there is an upside down letter "nun".

This, according to some commentaries, tells us that this passage is so important, it is a separate book of the Torah.

That would mean that there are not five, but seven books in the Torah: B'raishit, Shemot, Va'yikra, B'midbar chapters 1-10:34, Ba'midbar 10:35-36, B'midbar 11-36, and Devarim!

"We remember...the onions and garlic that we ate." (11:5)

Why did B'nai Yisrael complain that they didn't have these things if the mahn could taste like anything they wanted?

The Sifri says that the mahn didn't taste like onions and garlic because it's unhealthy for women who nurse their babies to eat onions and garlic.

TELL IT WITH A  The Torah says that Moshe was the most humble man on earth. A difficult characteristic to emulate.

A great Rabbi lay on his death bed. Surrounding him, were his loyal students.

"What virtue and piety our Rabbi has," one of them exclaimed.

"His brilliance is certainly incomparable," cried another.

"Yes, truly a wonderful man; kind and loving to his family and friends, even to total strangers," declared yet a third.

After going on and on about the Rabbi's greatness, they finally lapsed into silence. The Rabbi waited a minute or two and then asked, "What's the matter — about my humility you can't think of anything to say?"

GEMMATRIA **V'zeh ma'aseh ha'Menorah**, "And this is the workmanship of the Menorah" (8:4)

God tells Moshe how the Menorah should be made. The word *V'zeh* has the numeric value of 18. The Menorah was 18 handbreadth's high.

Moshe Sends Out Spies

God tells Moshe to send men to spy out the land of Canaan. Moshe is to send out the leaders of the tribes. The 12 spies include Yehoshua, whose name, Hoshea, Moshe now officially changes by adding a letter "yud."

Moshe tells the spies to check out the land. They are to report back on the strength of the people and the cities. They are to tell him if the land is good. They must also bring back samples of the produce of the land.

The Spies Return

After 40 days, the spies return with a giant cluster of grapes, pomegranates, and figs. They tell the people that the land flows with milk and honey. "But," they add, "the people are powerful and the cities are very fortified. We looked like grasshoppers when compared to the giants in the land."

The people hear this and begin to clamor to return to Egypt.

Calev, of the tribe of Yehuda, and Yehoshua, are the only ones who believe that the land is conquerable and that they should enter it and take it over.

But the people want to stone these two honest leaders.

Just then God's presence rests on the Ohel Moed.

Moshe Convinces God

God tells Moshe that rather than take B'nai Yisrael into a land they don't want, He will kill them all and make Moshe's descendents into a new nation.

Moshe pleads with God not to kill the people. He tells God that if He kills B'nai Yisrael, the nations of the world will say, "God was unable to bring the people into the Land that He swore would be theirs. Instead, He killed them in the desert."

God allows Himself to be convinced. He spares the lives of the nation. But "all those men who have tested Me these ten times and not listened to Me will not see the Land," God declares.

The punishment will be that B'nai Yisrael will have to continue wandering the desert. And, over the 40 years of wandering, all men who were 20 years or older when they left Egypt will die in the desert. This number, 40, coincides with the number of days the spies traveled through the Land of Israel.

The People Try to Enter the Land

The ten spies who gave a false report all died of a plague.

When the people realize what they have done and the punishment that they will receive, they decide to enter the land and conquer it.

But it is too late for them. They are no longer permitted to enter the Land. Moshe tells them to stop. But the people rush to enter the Land, are met by the enemy, and are beaten.

Challah

God tells Moshe to tell the people that when they reach the Land of Israel and want to eat bread, they have to set aside a portion of the dough for God. This portion should be from the first of the kneaded dough, and is to be performed for all generations.

The Wood Gatherer

Some of the people find a man gathering wood on Shabbat. They bring him to Moshe, Aaron, and the Sages. He is taken into custody, until Moshe finds out what to do with him.

God tells Moshe that the man is to be stoned to death.

Tzitzit

God tells Moshe to tell the people that they should make tzitzit on the corners of their clothing. This is also a commandment for all generations. They are also told to tie a thread of tehaylet — bluish colored wool — on the corner of their clothing.

The reason for the tzitzit is so that B'nai Yisrael will look at the tzitzit and remember to perform the commandments of God, rather than to go after the desires of their hearts and eyes.

The people are to remember too, that God took them out of Egypt.

TABLE TALK
DVAR TORAH

In our Parsha, God commands B'nai Yisrael to make tzitzit on the corners of their garments. The tzitzit must include a string of tehaylet, sky-blue wool. God explains that the purpose of putting on the tehaylet is to remember His commandments.

But what exactly is tehaylet?

The tehaylet is a dye that is extracted from a certain snail found in the ocean. For centuries, no one knew where to find this snail. So, people only wore the white strings of the tzitzit.

But if tehaylet is such an important component of tzitzit, why did people bother wearing tzitzit at all? Is doing half a mitzvah better than doing no mitzvah at all?

This question can be answered with the following parable:

There once was a great king who had two faithful family servants. He wanted to test their devotion so he summoned them to appear in front of him. He gave one servant a barrel and told him he had exactly 24 hours to fill the barrel with sand. The sand would be used for the king's garden. He gave the second servant an identical barrel and told him to fill it with as much pure gold as he could find within the next 24 hours. The gold would be used to fashion a new crown for the queen.

The following day both servants returned with empty barrels. Upon seeing this, the king became very upset with one of the servants.

Which servant do you think the king was upset with?

He was obviously upset with the servant who didn't bring back the sand. Sand is found everywhere and the servant's failure to fill the barrel showed that he couldn't care less about the king. However, the servant who didn't bring back the gold couldn't be faulted since he could hardly be expected to buy a barrel of gold with his servant's pay.

The same is true with tzitzit. When tehaylet does not exist, we are not expected to produce it out of thin air. But the white strings of the tzitzit, which are easy to obtain and an important part of the mitzvah, God expects us to obtain.

That is true of all God's commandments. We must do whatever we can to fulfill them.

WISDOM
OF THE
SAGES

The previous Parsha ends with Miriam being punished for speaking lashon hara, gossiping about Moshe. Why does the story of the spies come right after the story of Miriam?

The spies saw that Miriam was punished for speaking badly about Moshe, but still they did not take heed. They went to Canaan and returned, speaking badly about the Land of Israel. They should have learned a lesson from the story of Miriam, but they didn't.

When we refrain from speaking lashon hara, not only do we fulfill a mitzva, we also help unify the nation.

"Send for yourself..." (13:2)

Why does God add the words "for yourself", when speaking to Moshe? The Kli Yakar explains that God was hinting to Moshe that sending the spies would be for his own benefit. How?

God knew that the spies would sin, causing B'nai Yisrael to spend 40 years in the desert. Because he hit the rock, Moshe was destined to die before he entered the Land of Israel. So, by sending the spies, instead of dying right away, Moshe would get 40 extra years of life.

"And Moshe called Hoshea...Yehoshua." (13:16)

What's in a name...? Why did God want Moshe to change Hoshea's name?

In this case, a letter was added to his name. The *Yud* is a letter which represents God's name. God wanted to show everyone that His presence was with Yehoshua. Similarly, we find these name changes with Avraham and Sarah to show that God was with them as well.

 1) When the spies came back with news about the land, the nation heard two different versions. They elected to listen to the majority opinion. How could the nation be punished for listening to the majority opinion?

2) After the nation received their punishment, they wished to make amends by immediately fighting for the Land. Why didn't God let them?

3) After B'nai Yisrael are told that they would be wandering in the desert for 40 years, God gives them a few commandments that can only be fulfilled upon entering the Land of Israel. What's the purpose of giving them those commandments now?

4) On the second Shabbat after they received the Torah, B'nai Yisrael find the wood gatherer. There are those who say that he desecrated the Shabbat on purpose. What would be his reason for doing such a thing?

TELL IT WITH A SMILE

Friedman, a C.I.A. agent, was ordered to cross into Russia, and contact another agent by the name of Abrams.

The phrase with which they would be able to identify each other was, "It's ten o'clock, do you know where your children are?"

Under the cover of darkness, Friedman parachuted into the woods on the outskirts of Moscow.

He quickly discarded his parachute, and silently made his way to the address which he had memorized. When he reached the building, he realized that they had neglected to tell him in which apartment Abrams lived. Being a resourceful fellow, he checked the mailbox, where he was surprised to find two Abrams' listed. He went up to the first apartment and rang the bell.

When the occupant opened the door, Friedman asked, "Are you Abrams?"

"Yes I am," replied the man.

"Very good, then it's ten o'clock, do you know where your children are?" asked the agent.

"Oh no!" the other said. "I'm Abrams the mailman. You want Abrams the spy — he's on the third floor!"

GEMMATRIA

Our sages tell us that the commandment of tzitzit is equal to the whole Torah. How can we see this? The numeric value of tzitzit is 600. A corner of the tzitzit has eight strings and five knots. All in all, tzitzit in its entirety comes to 613, exactly the number of commandments in the Torah.

THE HAFTARAH CONNECTION

(Yehoshua 2:1-24)

In our Parsha, Moshe sends 12 people to spy out the Land of Israel. The spies bring back a negative report, and in doing so, convince the nation that the people in the land are too strong for them.

In the Haftarah, Yehoshua, who is now the leader of the nation, sends out two spies to spy out the city of Yeriho. Unlike the spies in our Parsha, these spies bring back a reassuring report, encouraging the nation to begin its attack.

The Rebellion of Korah

Korah, son of Yitzhar, grandson of Kehat and great grandson of Levi convinces Datan, Aviram and Ohn, from the tribe of Reuven, and 250 leaders of the people to confront Moshe and Aaron.

"You have too much power," the rebels say, accusingly. "We are all holy, so why do you two feel you have to act like our masters."

Moshe tells them that God will choose who should be the leader. They are to take pans with burning incense. From whomever God accepts the incense, that person will be the leader.

Moshe Rebukes the Rebels

Moshe tells Korah and the Levites that are with him that they should be satisfied with their position. Why do they want to be Kohanim too? Aaron has done nothing to merit such jealousy from them.

Then Moshe sends messengers to ask Datan and Aviram to come to him. But they refuse.

"Isn't it enough you brought us from a land flowing with milk and honey into the wilderness," they respond. "You want to control our lives too?"

The Rebels are Punished

Everyone meets at the Ohel Moed the next day. When all the pans are filled with burning incense, God's presence rests upon the Ohel Moed.

God tells Moshe and Aaron that He intends to destroy everyone, even those who stood by and let this rebellion happen. Moshe and Aaron plead with God not to destroy the many for the sins of the few.

God agrees. Moshe tells everyone to stay clear of the rebels, and the people draw back.

Then Moshe announces: "If these men die like regular people, then God is not with me. But if God creates something unique, a mouth from the ground that opens up and swallows them alive, then you know that these men have provoked God."

As soon as Moshe finishes speaking, a mouth from the ground opens up and swallows up Korah, his wealth, and all those who are with him.

Then a flame consumes the 250 men who were offering the incense.

A Covering for the Altar

God tells Moshe to tell Elazar, the son of Aaron, to collect all the pans of those who had been killed and melt them down, making a covering for the Altar.

This will serve as a reminder to the people that only the children of Aaron can bring incense to God.

A Terrible Plague

The people complain to Moshe and Aaron, accusing them of

killing the people of God. God tells Moshe again to move away and He will destroy everyone. Moshe and Aaron pray to save the people. Moshe knows that a plague has begun among the people and he sends Aaron with burning incense to provide atonement for them.

Aaron runs through the camp, standing between the dead and the living. The plague stops. But 14,700 people are dead of the plague.

The Eternal Staff of Aaron

God tells Moshe to tell the people that the leader of each tribe is to bring his staff. Every leader is to inscribe his name on his staff, and the name of Aaron is to be inscribed on the staff of Levi.

The staffs are then placed in the Ohel Moed. The next day when the staffs are inspected, the one with Aaron's name has blossomed, sprouting a bud and ripened almonds.

This staff is then placed in front of the Ark as a reminder to all those who want to rebel that rebellion only leads to death.

The Role of the Kohanim and Levites

The people are afraid that being close to the Mishkan will mean they will all die. God repeats the duties of the Kohanim and Levites in the Mishkan. It is they who bear the responsibility of the Mishkan, and it is they who are punished if the holiness of the Mishkan is in any way profaned.

God tells Aaron that it is his duty, and the duty of his children to be in charge of the sacrifices. Only they can eat of the terumah that is given by everyone. They are to get the best of all that grows, from the people. These holy offerings of B'nai Yis-rael are to be given to the Kohanim. This is the eternal *brit melach*, "the salt covenant," between God and Aaron and his descendants.

The Kohanim are also to get the firstborn of the kosher ani-mals and redeem the firstborn of some of the non-kosher ani-mals. Even the firstborn Children of Israel are to be redeemed. Five shekels are to be given to the Kohen for their redemption.

But in the Land of Israel, Aaron and his children will have no stake. God is their inheritance.

Likewise, the Levites are to depend on the people for their livelihood. They are to receive tithes from the people, but they will have no ownership in the Land.

Furthermore, the Levites will serve the Kohanim and be in charge of the Mishkan. They must give terumah to the Kohen from their tithes as well.

THE HAFTARAH CONNECTION

(Shmuel Book I 11:14-12:22)

In our Parsha, Korah rebels against the authority of Moshe and Aaron. He confronts them in front of the nation and demands that they step down.

In our Haftarah, B'nai Yisrael go to Shmuel, the prophet and leader of the people, and ask him for a king. They, like Korah, feel that a change in leadership is nec-essary. In this case too, God sees their request as an affront against His leadership. He is their true king.

TABLE TALK
DVAR TORAH

In the beginning of our Parsha, we read how Korah, together with over 250 others, tried to rebel against Moshe's leadership.

Korah's main complaint was that since the whole nation was holy, B'nai Yisrael didn't need one person to be singled out for greatness to rule over them.

The Midrash says that Korah tried to convince the nation by asking them two simple questions. The first question he posed was, "If a four-cornered garment is made out of tehaylet, does it need another string of tehaylet attached to it for a person to be considered as having fulfilled the commandment of wearing tzitzit?" He claimed that since the whole cloth was made of tehaylet, there is nothing that another string of tehaylet could add. So, why add it?

The second question he asked was, "Does a house full of Torah scrolls and other holy books, need a mezuza on the door?" His line of reasoning was that since whatever is written in the mezuza is already written in the Torah, there was no reason to have the mezuza singled out to be put on the door.

In the same vein, since all of B'nai Yisrael were holy, they didn't need to have someone holy put in charge of them.

At first glance, Korah's logic appears to make sense. A room full of Torah scrolls shouldn't need a mezuza, and a completely tehaylet cloth shouldn't need another tehaylet string attached to it.

But clearly, he was wrong. His punishment shows us how wrong he was.

It's not enough just to own an object of great importance. It has to be used, and even exhibited so that others will benefit from the object as well.

A piece of tehaylet cloth worn under one's garments, like a t-shirt, has limited effect upon the wearer. He soon forgets it is there. But a string of tehaylet dangling out of a shirt is a constant reminder of the mitzva of tzitzit and everything it represents.

The same is true of a house full of Torah scrolls. People won't notice the scrolls unless they walk into the house. But a mezuza can be seen, and touched even from the outside of the house.

That is also the purpose of having a leader for B'nai Yisrael. Left to their own devices, the Children of Israel might have languished in Egypt for many more years. They might have kept their holiness hidden from others and even themselves. But Moshe was able to draw out the holiness of the nation, and make it shine for all to see.

1) **Why were Korah's belongings also swallowed up forever?**

2) **Why was the test of leadership decided by bringing the incense in front of the Ohel Moed, and not by something else?**

3) **"The closer you get to God's presence, the more careful you have to be." How is this understood from this week's Parsha?**

Va'yigmol Sh'kaydim, "and almonds ripened" (17:23)

Aaron's staff sprouted almonds. The numeric value of the word *Sh'kaydim* is 454. That is the same numeric value as the word *Hashmonim*, the family of Kohanim who revolted against the Greeks and started the war that led to the miracle of Hanukkah. From here we see that Aaron sprouted not only almonds, but the future saviors and leaders of B'nai Yisrael.

WISDOM OF THE SAGES

"And the ground opened its mouth..." (16:32)

Rabbi Shalom Rokeah says that Korah and his followers were punished measure for measure. They rebelled by using their mouths to speak insolently to Moshe. Therefore, they were punished by a mouth swallowing them up.

The Mishna in Pirkay Avot 5:17 says: "Any disagreement that isn't for the sake of heaven will not last...what case is that? That is the argument of Korah and his followers."

When we argue, we must do so to defend the truth, not for selfish purposes, as was the case with Korah.

"And he put in the incense and it atoned for the nation." (17:12)

The Ba'al Ha'turim says that the incense was used here to stop the plague because B'nai Yisrael were now afraid of the incense. By stopping the plague with the incense, Aaron showed the people that it wasn't the incense that had killed the 250 rebels, but their sins. Used properly, the incense was a vehicle for good, not evil.

In his heart, Korah wanted to lead the people. He felt he could lead them blindly; forcing them to go wherever he wanted. Here's a story of two leaders who lead their flock "blindly."

Flight 766 was full and the passengers were waiting for the pilots. Needless to say, they were astonished when a man with dark glasses made his way on board, literally feeling his way to the cockpit. A second person, led by a seeing eye dog, arrived and also entered the captain's cabin.

The passengers were a bit nervous at first, but then they felt certain that this had all been the pilots strange sense of humor.

When the engines started up, the passengers watched as the plane headed down the runway.

But instead of lifting off, the plane kept speeding down the runway until the passengers could see the end of the runway fast approaching.

"Aieee!" they shouted. "Oh my God!" others chimed in.

The passengers now realized that the two blind pilots had not been joking. The closer the plane came to the end of the runway, the more hysterical the passengers became.

At the last moment, just as everyone was certain that the plane would overrun the runway, and as their screams reached new heights, the plane lifted off, just clearing the runway.

Meanwhile, in the cockpit, one pilot said to the other: "You know, one day the passengers will be too scared to scream, and then we'll never know when to take off."

The Red Cow

God tells Moshe and Aaron to tell the people about the red cow decree.

A red cow which has no blemish and has never had a yoke on it must be given to Elazar the Kohen. The cow is to be slaughtered, and Elazar is to sprinkle some of its blood seven times toward the Mishkan. The carcass is then totally burnt.

The Kohen who burns the cow has to immerse himself and his clothing, and wait until evening to become pure again. A pure person gathers the ashes of the cow and puts them in a designated place for safekeeping. This person has to immerse his clothing, and wait until evening to be pure again.

The Purifying Waters

The ashes of the red cow are mixed with water. Anyone who touches a corpse must have the purifying waters sprinkled on him before he can become pure again.

Miriam's Death and Moshe's Sin

The Children of Israel arrive in the Desert of Zin. Miriam dies and the people run out of water. They confront Moshe and complain, saying "Why did you take us out of Egypt to this terrible place? There's nothing to drink!"

God tells Moshe to take his staff, and together with Aaron and the people, he is to speak to the rock in front of them. Moshe will get water from the rock and the people and their animals will have what to drink.

Moshe gathers everyone before the rock and declares, "Listen, you rebels, you want us to bring water from this rock?" He lifts his staff and – instead of talking to the rock as God commanded – Moshe hits the rock twice. Water pours out of the rock and everyone drinks.

God tells Moshe and Aaron, "Because you did not believe in me enough to make my name holy among the people, you will not bring them into the Land that I have given them."

The King of Edom

Moshe sends messengers to the king of Edom asking to pass through the land of Edom. He promises to use only the highway and not to travel through private roads or fields. He also promises to pay for any water that the people or their animals may drink.

The king of Edom goes out to meet the Children of Israel with a large contingent of soldiers, barring the path of the Israelites. Left with no choice, the Children of Israel move on.

Aaron Dies

The Children of Israel arrive at Mount Hor. God tells Moshe and Aaron that Aaron will die on this mountain and not enter the Land of Israel because of what happened when Moshe hit the rock.

Moshe takes Elazar and Aaron up the mountain. He dresses

Elazar in Aaron's clothes. Then Aaron dies.

The people mourn Aaron for 30 days.

The Attack of the Snakes

The people become frustrated and complain about the lack of food and water. They also make light of the mahn, calling it, "worthless food."

God sends snakes to bite the people and many die. The people cry out, "We have sinned against God and Moshe!" And Moshe prays for them.

God tells Moshe to make the image of a snake on a pole. Whoever looks up at the snake is cured.

The Book of Wars of God

B'nai Yisrael traveled from place to place. A song is recorded in the Book of Wars of God about a well that God gave the people while they wandered in the desert.

The Amorites Attack

Moshe sends messengers to Sihon, king of the Amorites, asking to cross his land. Again, he promises not to trample anyone's property; not even to eat or drink anything that belongs to the Amorites.

But Sihon attacks. The Children of Israel destroy him and his army.

Then Og, king of Bashan, attacks. The Children of Israel destroy him and his people as well.

TABLE TALK
DVAR TORAH

O ur Parsha teaches us that someone who comes into contact with a dead body is impure. This impurity lasts for seven days, during which he undergoes a purification process. The ashes of the red cow is sprinkled on him during the third and seventh day. Afterwards, the impure person must immerse himself in water, and only then does he attain purity.

The procedure dealing with the red cow contains many laws. But there is one set of laws that seem to contradict each other.

On the one hand, the ashes of the cow is used as a purifying agent. But on the other hand, the Kohen who sprinkles the ashes, becomes impure.

How can the same ashes that purify one person, simultaneously cause another to become impure?

To give a really logical explanation for this contradiction is difficult because the Torah explicitly writes that this commandment is a "Hok" — a law without an explanation. Even King Solomon, who was gifted with supreme wisdom, admitted that of all the laws in the Torah, this is the only one he didn't understand.

Yet, while we may not understand the full reason for the red cow, we can learn at least one important lesson from it.

Giving of yourself demands more than merely the transfer of money from you to a poor person or charitable organization. Real giving, more often than not, contains an element of self sacrifice. When the Kohen sprinkles the ashes of the calf on a fellow Jew, he is giving of himself, of his ability. It is almost as if he is giving his friend some of his purity. This process depletes him of his own purity and he must therefore undergo a process of purification.

So, too, any true giving in life, whether by a teacher, a parent or a friend, involves some sort of sacrifice. Feeling depleted after you have given all you can is not a sign of weakness. On the contrary, it means you have transferred some of your essence to the other person, and in doing so have depleted your resources. As you replenish yourself, it is good to know that you have helped someone in need.

That feeling, that reward, is part of the purification process that will help you move forward.

WISDOM OF THE SAGES

"And Miriam died there...and there was no water to drink." (20:1-2)

From here our Sages learn that throughout the 40 years that B'nai Yisrael wandered in the desert, a well of water went with them. This well was given to them because of the merit of Miriam, Moshe's sister. When she died, the well dried up and the people began to complain about a lack of water.

Why was Aaron punished, after all he wasn't the one who hit the rock?

Our Sages say that the Torah purposely tells us that Moshe hit the rock twice. Had he hit it only once, Aaron would not have been blamed for contributing to Moshe's sin. But when Aaron saw Moshe lifting his hand to hit the rock a second time, he should have stopped him. For not doing so, he was punished as if he himself had hit the rock.

"The whole nation mourned Aaron for 30 days." (20:29)

We learn that everyone in the camp mourned for Aaron. He had touched the lives of men, women, young and old. How so?

The Midrash explains that Aaron was the consummate peacemaker. He was especially adept at making peace between a husband and wife. He would go to the husband and say that he had just spoken to his wife and that despite their argument, she still loved him very much. He would then go over to the wife and tell her the same things about her husband. When next they saw each other, husband and wife would rush to make up. It was this unique quality of being a true man of peace that made him beloved by all.

 **Lahen lo taveu et ha'kahal ha'zeh el ha'aretz**, "Therefore, you will not bring this nation to the Land." (20:12)

God tells Moshe and Aaron that since they didn't sanctify His Name, therefore they won't lead the congregation into Israel.

The numeric value of the word *Lahen* is one hundred. That is the same value as the phrase *Mida B'mida* which means, "measure for measure". Since by their sin they removed God's sanctity from B'nai Yisrael, so they will be removed from their positions of leadership and someone else will bring B'nai Yisrael into Israel.

 **1) Why were Moshe and Aaron punished so severely for hitting the rock? Certainly people have committed worse sins and received milder punishments.**

2) In our Parsha, two great people died. How do you think their deaths affected the nation?

3) In order to stop the plague, Moshe fashioned a copper snake on a pole. How could looking at a copper snake cure someone of his illness? Compare this to Shemot 17:11 where a similar question arises.

THE HAFTARAH CONNECTION

(Shoftim 11:1-33)

In our Parsha, B'nai Yisrael found it necessary to pass through different kingdoms on their way to Israel. One of these kingdoms was the kingdom of the Amorites. But Sihon, king of the Amorites, not only denied them permission, but took his army and attacked B'nai Yisrael.

In our Haftarah, Yiftah is requested to lead B'nai Yisrael in their fight against Ammon, the nation that now claims the land of the Amorites. Yiftah sends messengers to the king of Ammon and, basing himself on this week's Parsha, tells the king how B'nai Yisrael triumphed over Sihon and the Amorites. Yiftah warns the king of Ammon that the land B'nai Yisrael inhabits is rightfully theirs and that Ammon should stop picking fights with them.

TELL IT WITH A

Sometimes people are so thick headed you feel that instead of talking to them you'd like to give them a good...

Mr. and Mrs. Pitspop were discussing what to get their daughter for her eighth birthday. Finally, Mrs. Pitspop managed to convince her husband that a dog is just what little Annie needed.

On his way home from work, Mr. Pitspop stopped at a pet shop and asked for a dog.

The storekeeper told him that he had a special dog for him.

He went into the back room and came out holding a Pyrenees Mountain Dog.

"What's so special about him?" asked Mr. Pitspop.

"I'll tell you what's so special about him," said the store-keeper. "When you throw a stick in the water, this dog will fetch it without getting wet. He has the ability to walk on water!"

Mr. Pitspop thought for a moment and then said, "Forget it. I don't want him."

"Maybe you didn't hear me," the storekeeper said. "I told you he walks on water."

"I heard you," Mr. Pitspop assured him. "But tell me, who needs a dog that's too stupid to learn how to swim?"

בלק

THIS WEEK IN THE PARSHA

Balak asks Bilam to Curse the Israelites

Balak, king of Moav, hears what the Children of Israel did to the Amorites, and fears that they will destroy Moav too. He assembles the elders of neighboring Midyan. Together, they send messengers to the prophet, Bilam (also known as Balaam).

"Whomever you bless is blessed and whomever you curse is cursed," Balak's messengers tell Bilam. "So curse the Children of Israel for me."

The delegation of elders from Moav and Midyan come with presents to Bilam. He tells them to spend the night and in the morning he will tell them what God has said.

God tells Bilam not to curse the Children of Israel.

So, in the morning, Bilam sends the messengers back to Balak.

The Talking Donkey

Balak is persistent. He sends delegation after delegation. Finally, God allows Bilam to accompany a group of high ranking officers back to Balak. But Bilam is warned to do only what God tells him.

On the way, God sends an angel to stop Bilam. The donkey

sees the angel holding a sword, and veers off the path into a field. Bilam hits the donkey, trying to get it to go back onto the road.

But the angel blocks the donkey's path. The donkey is forced to walk into a vineyard which has a wall around it. In order to avoid the angel, the donkey presses against the wall, squeezing Bilam's leg against the wall as well. Bilam beats the donkey.

The donkey comes to a place where there is no room to turn around. The angel is in front of her, so she crouches down.

Bilam continues beating the donkey. The donkey starts to talk, saying, "Why did you hit me three times?"

Bilam answers, "Because you didn't listen to me. If I had a sword I would kill you."

"But haven't I always listened to you?" asks the donkey. "Have I ever done such a thing before?"

Bilam says, "No."

Then God reveals the angel to Bilam.

"You're fortunate that the donkey turned away from me," says the angel, "or I would have killed you, and let it live."

"I have sinned" Bilam admits. "If you want, I will return to my home."

The angel allows Bilam to continue, but reminds him, "only the words that God speaks to you will you say."

Bilam Blesses the Children of Israel

Bilam tells Balak that he can only say what God wants him to. One after another, they go to three different high places and set up seven altars in each place. But each time, instead of cursing the Children of Israel, Bilam blesses them with words like, "How good are your tents, Jacob, your dwelling places, Israel!"

Balak is frustrated, especially when Bilam admits he can only say what God tells him. So, Balak sends him home.

Pinhas the Zealot

The Children of Israel are in Shittim. The daughters of Moav and Midyan begin to entice the men, at the same time convincing them to worship the idol, Baal-peor.

A plague breaks out in the camp.

Moshe commands the judges of the people to kill anyone who practices such idolatry.

Suddenly, a man brings a Midyanite woman into the presence of Moshe and the people. Pinhas, the son of Elazar and grandson of Aaron the Kohen, takes a spear and follows the man and woman into a tent where he kills them.

The plague stops.

All told, 24,000 people have died from the plague.

FOOD FOR THOUGHT

1) Why did God ask Bilam to tell Him who the messengers of Balak were?

2) When Bilam fails to curse B'nai Yisrael, he decides to try a change of location. Why did he think that this new view would make a difference in his ability to curse the Jewish nation?

3) Pinhas, being a zealot, felt that he had to kill the two people who sinned in public. Is one ever permitted, even with the purest of intentions, to take the law into his own hands, or must the zealot be punished for his actions?

The beginning of our Parsha is very difficult to understand. Balak, the king of Moav, sends messengers to Bilam, and requests that he curse B'nai Yisrael. At first, Bilam acts correctly and asks permission from God before taking on such an endeavor. God's reply isn't difficult to anticipate. Bilam is told not to go with the messengers sent by Balak. God does not want him cursing His nation.

But Balak doesn't give up so easily. He sends other, more important people with greater gifts to try and persuade Bilam to take on the job of cursing B'nai Yisrael. When this high ranking delegation arrives, Bilam once again requests permission from God to go with them. Surprisingly, this time Bilam receives a positive answer. God tells him that he may go if he wants to, but he will have to say whatever God tells him to.

Why does God give Bilam two different answers?

This question arises again later on in the Parsha, when Bilam starts out on his journey to meet Balak. Bilam and his donkey encounter an angel. The angel tells Bilam that if it hadn't been for his donkey turning away, he would have killed Bilam. At this point Bilam actually volunteers to return home. But instead of sending him packing, the angel tells him that he can continue on his way, but that he must say what God tells him to.

If God doesn't want Bilam to go, why doesn't He tell him to do an "about face" and march home? If, on the other hand, God doesn't care if Bilam goes, why does the angel block Bilam's path? What is the purpose of these conflicting messages?

It is clear that God does not want Bilam to curse the Jewish people. God told Bilam that right away. Yet, just as Balak persisted in sending messengers, so Bilam persists in asking God for permission to go.

A person is led on the path he wishes to go. God knew that just as Balak would not take "no" for an answer, Bilam wasn't taking "no" for an answer either. So God let him go, with the warning that he was only to say the words God told him.

But Bilam felt he could outsmart God. He was sure he would find a way to curse the Jewish people. Whatever God told him, Bilam was sure he could twist to meet his own ends.

That's when God sends the angel. The angel is a warning that God knows the thoughts of man. Nothing is hidden from God. Having brought that point home, the angel allows Bilam to proceed.

And still Bilam persists. He goes from place to place with Balak, trying to find an "angle" from which to curse B'nai Yisrael. Finally, he realizes, and Balak realizes, that there is no tricking God. You may go to any height, to any extreme you want, but you can't change the will of God. And so Bilam ends up blessing B'nai Yisrael.

Our Sages tell us that "He who wishes to purify himself, is helped along." Had Bilam gone with the messengers in order to be a willing vehicle for God's words, he would have reaped rewards. God would have helped him. Instead, he went to get fame and wealth, and lost everything.

That is the lesson for all of us. We all have choices in our lives. God wants us to go on our path with bodies *and* with our minds and our hearts. Then God will help us along our way. And we will be successful.

Bilam had many opportunities and he let them pass him by. We must learn from this to take the opportunities we are offered and use them to make God's goals, our own.

GEMMATRIA **Hayn am l'vadad yishkon,** "They are a nation that dwells in solitude." (23:9)

Bilam blesses the Jews that they will dwell by themselves. When will this happen?

The numeric value of the phrase is 420, the same as the phrase *B'ymay Mashiah* which means, during the days of Messiah. Only then will B'nai Yisrael be left to live alone, undisturbed by its enemies.

WISDOM OF THE SAGES Bilam was as great a prophet among the other nations as Moshe was for B'nai Yisrael.

Why did God give the other nations such a great prophet?

Our Sages say that God didn't want the other nations to complain, saying, "If you had given us a Moshe we would have been great too!" So God gave them Bilam. But, unlike Moshe, he squandered his gift, spending his time trying to figure out how to outsmart God and curse the Jewish people.

"And Yisrael *settled* in Shittim... and the nation began to sin with the daughters of Moav." (25:1)

The Tractate Sanhedrin (106a) states that the word "settled" denotes sadness.

The Torat Haim explains that whenever B'nai Yisrael live outside of Israel, and put down roots in foreign soil, sadness is always bound to follow. For then they forget that the Land of Israel is their home and they are punished by God.

The Mishna in Pirkay Avot 5:6 relates that 10 things were created on the sixth day of creation, at twilight. One of these unique creations was Bilam's talking donkey.

It would appear that when God created the world, He made the natural order of creation – and the exeption to the rules of nature – all within the six days of creation.

As King Solomon days, "There is nothing new under the sun."

TELL IT WITH A

 *Balak must have thought that Bilam just didn't understand him. Every time he asked the prophet to curse the Jewish people, Bilam blessed them instead. Sort of like the communication problem described below.*

Who wrote the Gettysburg Address?" the teacher asked her class.

Barry, the class clown, shouted, "Not me!"

The students laughed hysterically. Tired of his senseless humor, the teacher told Barry that she wanted to see his father the following morning.

When Barry's father, a fairly new immigrant, met the teacher the following morning, she told him what his son had said.

"Well," began Mr Levi, "I know that Barry is no angel, but he isn't a liar either. If he says he didn't write it, then he didn't write it!"

Thinking Mr. Levi was teasing her, she dismissed him, saying, "I understand now where Barry gets his strange behavior from."

That night, when Mr. Levi told his wife the whole story, she reprimanded her husband for being so silly.

"Instead of defending our son, you should have apologized for Barry. Then you should have told the teacher that although Barry wrote it this time, he will never do it again!"

THE HAFTARAH CONNECTION

(Micha 5:6-6:8)

In our Parsha, Balak hires Bilam to curse B'nai Yisrael. But every time he tries to curse them, he ends up blessing them instead.

In the Haftarah, the prophet reprimands B'nai Yisrael for forgetting what happened with Bilam and Balak. The people have to realize that Bilam was sending a message to all Jewish generations. As long as they do the mitzvot, dwell together in peace, and pay homage to God, B'nai Yisrael are unconquerable.

God is not looking for mindless sacrifices from His people. Rather, He wants them to: "do justice, love kindness, and walk modestly with God." (6:8)

פינחס

The Pledge of Peace

The name of the man whom Pinhas killed was Zimri, the prince of the Tribe of Shimon. The name of the woman was Kozbi, a princess of the Midyanites.

God tells Moshe that Pinhas was a zealot in avenging God and his act saved the Children of Israel from destruction. "Therefore," God announces, "I give him My pledge of peace."

From now on Pinhas and all his descendants will be Kohanim, because Pinhas "atoned for the Children of Israel."

As far as the Midyanites are concerned, God commands Moshe to destroy them at every opportunity.

A New Census

After the plague, God tells Moshe and Elazar to take a census of all the men 20 years and older. The total number is 601,730.

The male Levites are counted separately, from one month old. Their total is 23,000.

None of the men counted are part of the original exodus from Egypt. As God decreed, they all died in the desert, except for Calev and Yehoshua.

Division of the Land

God tells Moshe that the Land of Israel will be divided according to the census. Large families will receive a greater portion than small families. A special lottery will be used to determine the portion that each of the Twelve Tribes will get in the Land.

The Daughters of Tzelofhad

The five daughters of Tzelofhad, from the Tribe of Menashe, come to Moshe and everyone in the camp who was at the Ohel Moed.

"Our father died in the desert," they say, "and he was not part of the rebellion of Korah. He had no son. Why should our family not get an inheritance in the Land. Just because he had no son?"

Moshe asks God for guidance. God tells him, "The daughters of Tzelofhad are right. They should get the inheritance of their father in the Land.

"And tell the people that if a man doesn't have a son, then his daughter receives his inheritance. If he has no daughter, then the man's brothers receives his inheritance. If he has no brothers, then give the inheritance to his father's brother. If there are no brothers of his father, give it to the closest relative."

God concludes by saying, "This is a decree of justice for the Children of Israel."

Moshe Asks For A Replacement

God tells Moshe to go up the mountain of Avarim and see the Land of Israel. Because he sinned by hitting the rock, Moshe will not go into the Land.

But Moshe wants God to appoint someone to replace him.

God says, "Take Yehoshua and lean your hands on him. Stand him in front of Elazar and the people and command him in front of them. You will place some of your greatness on him, so that everyone will listen to him."

The Holiday Sacrifices in the Mishkan

A twice daily Tamid sacrifice has to be brought in the Mishkan in the morning and evening.

Additional holiday sacrifices have to be brought on Shabbat, Rosh Hodesh, Pesah, Shavuot, Rosh Ha'shana, Yom Kippur, Sukkot, and Shemini Atzeret.

THE HAFTARAH CONNECTION

(Melahim I; 18:46-19:21)

In our Parsha, Pinhas is acknowledged as the first zealot of the Jewish nation. It was this quality which compelled him to take action, and kill the two sinners.

In our Haftarah, we see that this quality still exists within B'nai Yisrael and is one of the characteristics of a great prophet. As Eliyahu says (19:10,14): "I have indeed been very zealous for God."

TABLE TALK
DVAR TORAH

The question arises, why was Pinhas rewarded for acting zealously, with God's "Covenant of Peace"? There were many other rewards God could have given Pinhas. Why was this covenant singled out?

In order to understand the reward of Pinhas, we must first understand what it means to be a Kohen, a descendant of Aaron. What is the function and nature of Kehunah?

Aaron was chosen as the first Kohen because he "loved peace and pursued peace." (Pirkay Avot 1:12). Aaron was the first recipient of the "Nobel Peace Prize," as it were. He devoted his life to the ideal of peace, never considering it beneath his dignity to foster love and understanding, even when the press cameras weren't rolling. He pursued peace between man and man; and thus, it was fitting that he continue his role of peacemaker in the Sanctuary becoming the Kohen Gadol, the lightning rod for shalom between man and man *and* man and God.

Aaron came to symbolize the ideal Kohen; the man of God who is, above all, a man of peace; one who strives for the welfare of others with no thought of personal gain.

Pinhas put his own life at risk when he rushed into Zimri's tent. He did this because there was a plague ravaging the nation. God commends Pinhas for atoning for the Jewish people. Pinhas acted to bring about peace between man and God just like a Kohen who serves in the Sanctuary. His desire to create shalom between man and God showed that he was worthy of the enormous responsibility of fostering peace and understanding within the nation.

Aaron's overriding quality was his selfless desire to create shalom between man and man. Pinhas was selected for preserving the connection between man and God. Both these approaches demonstrate a love for the people. That love is the trademark of a Kohen.

Can we, who are termed a "kingdom of Kohanim", fail to exhibit that same love to God and towards each and every member of our nation?

WISDOM OF THE SAGES Pinhas managed to halt God's anger from B'nai Yisrael by killing the perpetrators, and in return, he received the covenant of peace. The word peace, *shalom* in Hebrew, is written with the letter *vav*. In the Torah, this particular vav is written with a small gap between the top and the rest of the letter. God wanted to show us, that although peace was achieved, it wasn't complete because two people died in the process. Every life is sacred.

The Midrash tells us that the daughters of Tzelofhad received their inheritance because, unlike the men of that generation, they always insisted on continuing the journey toward the Land of Israel. Once they entered the Land, it would have been unfair for their father's inheritance to be given away after they worked so hard to achieve this goal.

"One sheep shall be brought in the morning, and a second sheep in the afternoon." (28:4)

Every day in the Mishkan, two sheep had to be brought, one in the morning and another in the afternoon.

This is the hallmark of the Jew: To be consistent in his devotion to the commandments, and to make them always seem new to him no matter how often they have to be done.

1) Why is it important for us to know who it was that Pinhas killed?

2) For the second time in the book of B'midbar, B'nai Yisrael are counted. Why now?

3) What are the criteria Moshe expects from a leader. Does it have anything to do with his own past?

TELL IT WITH A SMILE

God promised Pinhas "a covenant of peace." The prophet Yeshayahu said that one day there will be universal peace, when "the lamb will lie down with the lion."

One fine Sunday, Berel decided to go to the local zoo with his wife and kids.

As he neared the lion's cage, he was astonished to see a lamb lying peacefully with a lion beside her.

"That's wonderful," he cried. "Finally, Yeshayahu's prophecy is realized!"

Berel ran to the zookeeper. "My congratulations! You have finally made everyone see that peace is at hand. But tell me," he implored of the zookeeper, "how do you make the lion lie down with the lamb?"

"It's no problem," replied the zookeeper. "Every morning, I simply put another lamb in the lion's cage!"

Meh'hodha, "from your glory." (27:20)

In passing leadership to Yehoshua, Moshe was commanded to transfer his glory to his assistant. The numeric value of *Meh'hodha* is 75. That is the same value as the word *Ha'sod,* "the secret." From here we learn that Moshe also passed on many secrets of creation to Yehoshua.

מטות

THIS WEEK IN THE PARSHA

Making Vows

Moshe tells the heads of the tribes of B'nai Yisrael that a man must honor his vows, whether it is a vow to God or a vow to prohibit something to himself.

If a young girl vows, her father can negate her vow. If her father hears her vow, but decides to ignore it, she has to keep her vow. Similarly, if a wife vows, her husband can negate her vow. But if he keeps silent during her vow, then she has to keep it.

Vengeance Against Midyan

God tells Moshe to avenge B'nai Yisrael by attacking the Midyanites.

Moshe takes 1,000 men from each tribe and appoints Pinhas as their leader. B'nai Yisrael kill the kings of Midyan, Bilam, and all the males of the nation. They return with female captives and young children, as well as with all the wealth of the Midyanites.

Moshe is angry with them for keeping the women alive. "At Bilam's suggestion, they caused the Children of Israel to betray God at Peor. So kill the women who are not virgins, and all the male children."

Laws of Koshering Vessels

Elazar the Kohen teaches the soldiers who have been in battle the laws of koshering utensils. All metal vessels which have come into contact with fire have to be koshered by putting them through fire. They must also be purified by having the "water of sprinkling," the combination of water and ashes from the red cow, sprinkled on them. Vessels that have not come into contact with fire are to be immersed in water.

Dividing the Spoils

God tells Moshe to divide the spoils in half, between those who went to battle and the rest of the people.

From the spoils of the soldiers, one captive and one animal in 500 is to be given to Elazar as teruma. From the people, one captive and one animal in 50 is to be given to the Levites.

The commanders of the army report that there were no casualties. In appreciation of this fact, they bring all the jewelry they have captured to Moshe and Elazar. It is taken to the Ohel Moed.

The East Bank of the Jordan

The leaders of the tribes of Reuven and Gad come to Moshe, Elazar, and the heads of the people. These tribes have a great deal of livestock and want to settle on the east bank of the Jordan River.

Moshe thinks that they don't want to fight in the upcoming battles for the Land of Israel and he becomes angry. But they correct this false impression at once.

"We only want to build corrals for our animals and cities for our children," they explain. "Then we will lead the battle to make sure each tribe receives its inheritance in the Land."

Moshe agrees. "Build cities for your children and corrals for your flock," he tells them, "and do what you have said you will do."

Moshe gives the tribes of Reuven, Gad, and half the tribe of Menashe cities on the east bank of the Jordan River.

1) Why was God so adamant about destroying Midyan (31:2)? What is the reason that Moshe gives (31:3)? What does this show us about the relationship between God and His nation?

2) The booty from the war with Midyan was to be divided between the nation and the warriors. Why should those who didn't fight receive a portion?

3) The tribes of Reuven and Gad told Moshe that they would build pens for their cattle and cities for their children. Moshe told them to build cities for their children and then pens for their cattle. What does the order show about the difference in their values?

GEMMATRIA

Vi'lo nifkad me'menoo ish, "...and not one man was missing." (31:49)

After the war with Midyan, B'nai Yisrael found that not one of their number had been killed. This was a sign that none of the fighters had sinned during the battle by losing his faith in God.

The numeric value of the phrase *Vi'lo nifkad me'menoo ish* is 718. The numeric value of the word *La'avairot*, which means, "for sins" is also 718. Thus none of the fighters had fallen because of his sins.

TABLE TALK
DVAR TORAH

In our Parsha, we find that Pinhas and the rest of the Israeli warriors triumph over the Midyanites. Upon returning to camp, they are faced with the problem of how to purify the booty they have taken.

Elazar tells them, *Zot hukat ha'Torah...,* "This is the decree of the Torah" as to how to purify utensils. He then explains the simple process which would enable them to use the vessels. Any vessel that could withstand heat, had to be purified by being placed in fire, and then sprinkled with the special waters of purification. Any vessel that did not come into contact with fire was to be immersed in water.

Rabbi Moshe Feinstein points out that the phrase, *Zot hukat ha'Torah* appears in only one other place in the Torah. The phrase is used in connection to the *para aduma*, the red cow. The para aduma is considered the most puzzling of all Jewish laws. It is so complex, that even King Solomon was forced to admit, "I said I will be wise, but it was far from me."

Why does the Torah make use of this phrase in both the seemingly simple commandment in our Parsha, and in the baffling one pertaining to the red cow?

By equating these two issues, the Torah is telling us that they are both the same in one very important way. For, even though one seems simple and the other inexplicable, we have, in fact, no greater understanding of one than the other.

That is true of all God's commandments. Even if we think we understand some of the mitzvot, there are many facets within them which are hidden from us, facets which we will never be aware of. It is for this reason that we must fulfill God's commandments whether or not we think we understand them.

WISDOM OF THE SAGES

"Take revenge for B'nai Yisrael against Midyan..." (31:2)

Moshe receives a commandment from God to avenge B'nai Yisrael. However, instead of leading the battle himself, he sends Pinhas. Why didn't he go himself?

Moshe was raised in Midyan, so he felt a certain gratitude towards them. It would have been difficult for him to lead the army against the nation who had raised him. However, since Pinhas had killed the Midyanite woman who had sinned with Zimri, Moshe felt he would be the right one to finish the job.

"A band of sinning people." (32:14)

Our sages tell us that God got very angry with Moshe for referring to B'nai Yisrael in such a negative manner.

As a result, Moshe was eventually punished, and one of his descendants – Yonatan ben Gershom – went on to worship idols.

We can see from here how careful we must be with our wording, even if what we say is valid.

TELL IT WITH A SMILE

Pinhas was the first in a tradition of great Jewish generals.

After the Six Day War, President Nixon called up Prime Minister Golda Meir of Israel and asked her if she would be willing to trade General Moshe Dayan for any three American generals of her choice.

Golda readily agreed.

"We'll give you General Dayan," she told the President, "for your top three generals: General Motors, General Electric, and General Telephone!"

THE HAFTARAH CONNECTION

(Yermeyahu 1:1-2:3)

This is the first of the three "prophecies of destruction," read during the *Three Weeks*, that period of time between the Fasts days of the Seventeenth of Tamuz and the Ninth of Av.

This Haftarah is usually read on the Shabbat following the Fast of the Seventeenth day of Tamuz. It reminds us why we fast on the Seventeenth of Tamuz and the Ninth of Av. Yermeyahu has a vision in which he sees a pot spilling its contents. For him, this is a sign that B'nai Yisrael will soon have to succumb to their enemies. Since, in his vision, the pot spills towards the north, it is a sign that trouble will develop from there, which is where the Babylonian exile eventually takes place.

מסעי

The Borders of the Land of Israel

Moshe reviews the 42 places B'nai Yisrael camped during their wanderings in the desert.

Then God tells Moshe the borders of the Land of Israel.

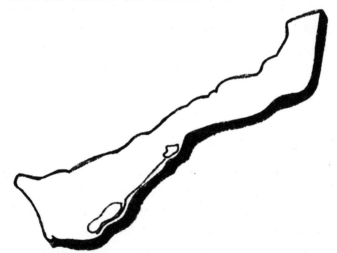

Southern Border – The Desert of Zin, the edge of the Dead Sea, Atzmon, the southern part of the Mediterranean Sea.

Northern Border – The Mediterranean Sea, Mount Hor, Zedad, Hazar-enan.

Eastern Border – Hazar-enan, Riblah, the Kinneret, the Jordan River, the Dead Sea.

Western Border – The Mediterranean Sea.

The Cities of the Levites

God tells Moshe that when the Children of Israel receive their inheritance in the Land of Israel, they are to give the Levites cities to live in. There are to be 48 Levite cities in all. Each city is to have open space around it as well as land for cultivation.

The Cities of Refuge

Of the 48 cities to be given to the Levites, six are to be cities of refuge. Three will be built on the eastern side of the Jordan River and three on the western side of the Jordan River. A person who kills someone by accident can seek refuge in the cities of refuge. Once in the city, the murderer cannot be harmed by the people who wish to avenge the death of the person he murdered.

The Murderer

If a person kills someone intentionally with an object, like a rock, that could cause death, he is a murderer and must be put to death. If a person kills someone out of hatred, or ambushes him, he is a murderer and must be put to death. In both cases, a family member, seeking revenge for the murder, may kill the murderer if he finds him.

But someone who kills unintentionally, or with an instrument, like a pebble, that normally would not cause death, then the judges must rescue the person from the hands of the avenger and bring him to trial. If he is innocent of intentional murder, the person is sent to a city of refuge where he has to live until the Kohen Gadol dies. Should he ever leave the city, the avenger can kill him. After the death of the Kohen Gadol, the person can go back to his home, without fear of being killed.

If a person kills someone and there are two witnesses who testify, the person must die. But one witness cannot convict a person in a murder case.

The court cannot accept money to allow a convicted murderer to live. Nor can they accept money to allow an unintentional murderer to leave the city of refuge before the Kohen Gadol dies.

Marriage and Inheritance

The leaders of the Tribe of Menashe approach Moshe and the leaders of the other tribes. They are concerned that if the daughters of Tzelofhad marry outside their tribe, they will take their inheritance with them, thereby decreasing the property of the Tribe of Menashe. They are aware that even when the Yovel arrives, and all land is returned to its original owner, the land that the daughters of Tzelofhad take with them will not return back to the tribe.

Moshe tells them that the daughters of Tzelofhad are to marry only within the Tribe of Menashe. An inheritance should not leave the tribe it comes from. Rather, any woman who inherits must marry within her tribe.

The five daughters of Tzelofhad married men within the Tribe of Menashe.

1) Why does Moshe record all of the places where B'nai Yisrael stopped?

2) The Levites lived in the cities of refuge all year round. Why were they chosen to inhabit these cities?

3) There were three cities of refuge on either side of the Jordan. Yet on one side, there were two and a half tribes and on the other, nine and a half. Doesn't this seem disproportionate?

WISDOM OF THE SAGES

"These are the journeys of B'nai Yisrael..." (33:1)

The seventh letter in the Hebrew alphabet, *Zayin,* is missing from the section detailing the journeys of B'nai Yisrael.

This comes to teach us that B'nai Yisrael never journeyed on Shabbat, the *seventh* day of the week.

Our Parsha explains that the Kohen Gadol's death is the only way out of a city of refuge. In the Tractate Makot 11a, we read that the Kohen Gadol's mother used to go to the different cities of refuge, and give out food to the murderers. This was done as a sort of bribe so that they wouldn't pray for her son's death.

❖

"And they moved from the Sinai Desert, and they camped at Kivrot Ha'ta'ava." (33:16)

Kivrot Ha'ta'ava means "burial place of desire."

Rabbi Tzvi Pesah Frank says that from here we can learn that if we move away from Sinai, meaning the Torah, then we will end up succumbing to our desires. The Torah is what helps us keep our desires in check.

TABLE TALK
DVAR TORAH

In our Parsha, we learn the laws of the *Aray Miklat,* the cities of refuge. This is a special place designated for anyone who kills a fellow Jew unintentionally. The killer has to get to the city of refuge before the deceased's relatives are able to avenge his death.

With regard to the killer's release from the city, we find a very peculiar law. He may only leave the city without fear of being hunted down, after the Kohen Gadol of that time, dies.

What is the connection between the Kohen Gadol's death and the killer's atonement? Why should his release be dependant on the death of the Kohen Gadol?

In order to understand this relationship, we must first understand how the killer found himself in his predicament.

In the Parsha of Mishpatim (Shemot 21:13) we already learned that if someone kills unintentionally, he will have to run to a city of refuge. Rashi explains that the case we are discussing is one in which two men commit murder, one intentionally and one unintentionally. Since there are no witnesses to either murder, they are both acquitted.

God, however, does not acquit them. He creates the following scenario: One day, the man who had killed unintentionally climbs up a ladder, and the man who had killed intentionally is at the foot of the ladder. The man at the top of the ladder falls and kills the one below, but this time, in front of witnesses. Now, the man who had originally murdered on purpose meets with his just punishment — death, and the one who had killed by accident is now forced to run to a city of refuge.

The end result here is that for every person that goes to an *Ir Miklat,* two people are killed! This is definitely a reflection of the poor spiritual state in which the nation finds itself. The abundant number of murders is a direct result of failing to follow God's path.

Now we are in a better position to understand why the atonement of the unintentional killer comes with the death of the Kohen Gadol. It is because the Torah holds the leaders of the nation responsible for the spiritual well-being of the nation, not only on a theoretical scale, but even on a specific individual level.

The Kohen Gadol was not spiritual enough, or did not work hard enough to create the spiritual life that B'nai Yisrael needed to overcome their negative impulses. Therefore, a murder, even an unintentional murder, is the Kohen Gadol's responsibility.

THE HAFTARAH CONNECTION

(Yermeyahu 2:4-28, 3:4)

This is the second of the three "prophecies of destruction," read during the *Three Weeks,* that period of time between the Fast days of the Seventeenth of Tamuz and the Ninth of Av.

Our Haftarah keeps to the theme of the Three Weeks by showing us Yermeyahu rebuking the nation. He chastises them for making a mockery of the Land and the Torah. People are ignorant of the Torah, and false prophets spread their lies throughout the Land.

 The numeric value of the first two locations that B'nai Yisrael traveled records the history of B'nai Yisrael from the time of Avraham until King Solomon.

The first place, *Ramses*, has the numeric value of 430, which is the number of years from the time of the *Brit Bain Ha'betarim,* the covenant God made with Avraham, until the Exodus.

The second place, *Sukkot,* has the numeric value of 480, which is the number of years between the Exodus and the building of The First Temple.

 *In our Parsha, God defines the laws of the cities of refuge by giving examples of those who would have to go to these cities. When it comes to defining emotions, however, sometimes you have to do more than just list examples.*

David was having trouble understanding some of the more difficult words in the story, so he asked his father for some help. "What's the difference between anger and exasperation?" he inquired.

Mr. Gold, David's father, picked up the phone. "Now you pick up the other phone," he told his son, "and you'll hear the difference." He then dialed a random number.

"Hello, is David there?" Mr. Gold asked the man who picked up the phone.

"Mister," the man answered, "there's no David here. Next time look up the number before you dial!" Then the man hung up.

"You see," Mr. Gold said, "that man was slightly exasperated."

He then dialed the same number, and again asked to speak to David.

"Now listen," came the heated reply, "I already told you that David doesn't live here. You better not dial this number again!" The man slammed the receiver down, hard.

David's father turned to his son and said, "Now I'll show you the difference between exasperation, and true anger."

For the third time, he dialed the man's number and when the voice on the other side roared out a violent "Hello!" Mr. Gold calmly replied, "Hello, this is David. Any calls for me?"

THE BOOK OF
DEVARIM

THIS WEEK IN THE PARSHA

A simple, straightforward exposition
of the weekly reading.

TABLE TALK
DVAR TORAH

A brief, cogent talk about the
weekly reading that can be
repeated at the Shabbat table.

FOOD FOR THOUGHT

Questions and concepts for
you to think about.

GEMMATRIA

Discusses the numerical value
of words found in the Parsha.

WISDOM
OF THE
SAGES

Rabbinic pearls of wisdom.

THE HAFTARAH CONNECTION

Explains how the Haftarah
connects to the weekly Parsha.

TELL IT WITH A

SMILE

A short humorous anecdote
that relates to the Parsha.

דברים

Forty Years in Review

On the first day of the 11th month, in the 40th year of their wandering in the desert, Moshe begins to review what B'nai Yisrael have been through.

The Judges

"I told you," Moshe reminds the people, "that I alone could no longer shoulder the responsibility of settling all your problems. So I appointed judges over you, the best and the brightest among you, to judge righteously. I told the judges to be careful not to show any favoritism to anyone, nor be afraid of anyone. And I instructed the judges that any case too difficult for them to judge should be brought to me."

The Spies

"When we left Horev," Moshe continues, "and were about to enter the Land, I said to be brave and not lose heart.

"But you asked that spies first enter the Land. I liked that idea and took one man from each tribe to spy out the Land. They returned with good news about the bounty of the Land. But you all rebelled, listening only to the negative reports about the mighty strength of those who live on the Land.

"I tried to tell you not to fear the other nations. But you refused to believe in God."

Then Moshe recalls how God became angry and swore that none of that generation would enter the Land, except Calev and Yehoshua who, after all, had pleaded with the people not to rebel and to enter the Land.

When the people heard that they would not be able to enter the Land, they rebelled again by trying to rush into the Land, only to be beaten by the Amorites.

The Children of Esav

Moshe recounts how the people passed through the land of Seir where the descendants of Esav lived. The children of Esav feared B'nai Yisrael, but the Children of Israel were not permitted to provoke them. They could only buy food and drink from them.

Moav and Ammon

Since the nations of Moav and Ammon were descended from Lot, Avraham's nephew, B'nai Yisrael were not permitted to conquer their land.

Sihon and Og

Sihon, Moshe recalls, was the Amorite king who would not allow B'nai Yisrael to pass through his land. He attacked them and the Children of Israel destroyed him and occupied his cities.

Og, king of Bashan, a giant among men, also attacked B'nai Yisrael and was destroyed. All his cities were occupied by the

Children of Israel as well.

The tribes which occupied the land of Sihon and Og were Reuven, Gad, and half the tribe of Menashe. These two-and-a-half tribes were permitted to live on the eastern bank of the Jordan River as long as they helped conquer the rest of the Land of Israel.

THE HAFTARAH CONNECTION

(Yeshayahu 1:1-27)

This is the third and last of the "prophecies of destruction," which are read during the three weeks between the Fast of the Seventeenth of Tamuz and the Fast of the Ninth of Av.

This Haftarah is read the Shabbat before the Ninth of Av, the day the First and Second Temples were destroyed.

This is a most fitting Haftarah for the occasion. The vision Yeshayahu had clearly shows what was expected of B'nai Yisrael, and to what level they had sunk.

In order to save the nation from itself, the destruction of both the State and the Temple was necessary.

The Haftarah ends by giving us the formula for deliverance: "Zion will be redeemed by justice..." (1:27)

GEMMATRIA

Aileh Ha'devarim... (1:1) "These are the words..."

The book of Devarim is a collection of speeches that Moshe delivered before he dies. These speeches lasted for 36 days, from the first of Shevat until the seventh of Adar.

This is hinted to in the word *Aileh*, "these," which has the numeric value of 36.

TABLE TALK
DVAR TORAH

"These are the words which Moshe spoke to all Israel." (1:1)

This is how the fifth and final book of the Torah begins. In this book, Moshe rebukes the Jewish people, admonishes them for what they have done, and charges them to keep the Torah in the future.

When we look at the beginning of the Parsha, it's hard to understand what it is Moshe wants from the nation. He mentions a number of different places the people camped, but what, if anything, is the relationship between these places and B'nai Yisrael?

Rashi says that Moshe is listing all the places where B'nai Yisrael had sinned in the past.

But why didn't Moshe just admonish B'nai Yisrael outright, telling them what they did wrong, instead of hinting to it by reciting the names of the places?

Moshe wanted to get his message across to B'nai Yisrael, but in a subtle way, so as not to cause them any embarrassment in the process. The people knew only too well what had happened – what sins they had committed – at the places Moshe mentioned. They didn't have to be hit over the head, a hint was enough.

From the way Moshe spoke, we can learn an important lesson when it comes to dealing with people.

Nobody is perfect. We all sin on occasion. But when someone sins, it's not right to bluntly confront him with his terrible act. Rather than causing remorse, such confrontation may cause the person tremendous embarrassment, and may even lead to dreadful consequences.

The Tractate Gittin (57) recounts the story of two people,

Kamtza and Bar Kamtza, and states that because Kamtza embarrassed Bar Kamtza in public, God ultimately, allowed His Temple to be destroyed!

That's why Moshe only alluded to the sins of the people. That is the way to successfully help others learn from their mistakes.

WISDOM OF THE SAGES

"May the God of your forefathers increase your numbers a thousandfold, and bless you as He has told you." (1:11)

Why was it necessary for Moshe to add on at the end "and bless you as He has told you?"

Rashi says that when B'nai Yisrael heard that they would be increased a thousandfold, they were upset. God had already promised them they would be so numerous that they couldn't be counted at all!

This sentence tells us that Moshe's blessing was that they multiply "a thousandfold." As for God's blessing, "(He should) bless you as He has told you."

"And God heard the voice (sound) of your words, and became angry." (1:34)

When Moshe talks about God's reaction to the spies' report, why did he add the word "voice"?

To teach us that the words a person utters are not always a the real message. Many times it is the tone of a person's voice that tells us if his statement is positive or negative.

The tone of voice that the spies used, even when listing the good things about the Land, was very negative. God was angry with them not only because of their words, but because of their "voice" as well.

At the end of the Parsha, we come across the death of Og, the king of Bashan.

Who was Og?

The Me'am Loez says that he was the last of the race of giants who lived during the time of the Flood. He was saved by hanging on to the Ark. Noah gave him food, and Og became his slave. He was then given to Nimrod, who gave him to Avraham. Avraham eventually set him free.

Og eventually became the King of Emor, and was killed by Moshe when he decided to fight B'nai Yisrael.

1) How could Moshe tell B'nai Yisrael that they were "as numerous as the stars," if, at the time, the men that were counted only numbered 600,000?

2) Moshe wanted the "smart and wise" people to step forward to judge the people. Is there a difference between smart and wise? If so, what is it?

3) Compare Moshe's recounting of the story of the spies, to the way it is written in B'midbar 13. Find at least two differences. Did Moshe "forget" what really happened, or did he relay it in this fashion for a reason?

Moshe had difficulty coping with the everyday complaints of the people, so he appointed judges. Some people have their own unique way of solving their problems...

After many years as chief of surgery at a major hospital, Doctor X finally succumbed to the enormous pressures of the job and had to be taken from his office in a straightjacket to a psychiatric hospital.

It took eight years, but at long last he was pronounced cured. While he was packing, Dr. Y, the head of the medical team that had evaluated him, paid him a visit and asked him what he intended to do once he returned to sociey.

Dr. X answered, "Well, as your records show I am not only an M.D. but a chiropractor as well. I can, no doubt, open up an office and begin working. If that proves unprofitable, I am also an engineer and can always work for one of the big companies. If that too proves to be a dead end, I have a Ph.D. in Business Management and can always start my own business.

"So as you see, I am not only completely recovered, but I have many ways in which to earn a living."

"But suppose none of them are successful?" asked Dr. Y.

"In that case," Dr. X answered smartly, "I can always be a teapot!"

ואתחנן

THIS WEEK IN THE PARSHA

Moshe's Plea to God

After conquering Sihon and Og, Moshe reminds B'nai Yisrael that he pleaded with God to let him enter the Land of Israel.

"Let me please cross and see the good Land on the other side of the Jordan River," I asked God.

"But God became angry with me because of you," Moshe tells the people. "God said, 'It is too much for you! Don't talk about it anymore. Go to the top of the cliff and look to the west, north, south, and east. You will see the Land, but you will not cross the Jordan.' I was told that Yehoshua was going to take the people to the Land that I saw."

Moshe Warns the People

Moshe tells B'nai Yisrael what to do when they enter the Land of Israel.

"Do not add to the words that I commanded you, nor subtract from them," Moshe says. "For which nation has a God who is so close to it, and answers whenever He is called?

"But beware," Moshe warns them, "that you don't forget the things your eyes saw, nor remove from your hearts that which you witnessed all the days of your life."

The Prophecy of Exile and Redemption

"When you have been in the Land a long time," Moshe tells them, "you will become corrupt and worship idols thereby provoking God's anger." He then calls the heavens and earth to serve as witnesses to the fact that if B'nai Yisrael do practice idol worship, they will be thrown out of the Land.

"You will be scattered by God to all the nations, and you will be few in number. There you will serve the gods of wood and stone."

But eventually, Moshe assures them, "You will seek God and you will find Him, if you search for Him with all your heart and all your soul. In the end of days, you will return to God and listen to His voice."

Finally, Moshe tells them, "You must observe God's decrees and His commandments, so that you will prolong your days on the Land that God gives you, forever."

Moshe Sets Aside the Cities of Refuge

Moshe then sets aside three cities of refuge on the West Bank of the Jordan River: Betzer, Ramot, and Gilad. They are to be used by a person who accidentally kills another person.

The Ten Commandments

Moshe reminds the people what happened at Mt. Sinai; how he stood between them and God, because they were afraid of the fire that lit up the mountain. He then repeats the Ten Commandments:

169

1. I am your God, Who took you out of Egypt, from slavery.
2. You shall not make images for worship.
3. You shall not take God's Name in vain.
4. Keep the Shabbat day holy.
5. Honor your father and your mother.
6. You shall not kill.
7. You shall not commit adultery.
8. You shall not steal.
9. You shall not bear false witness against your neighbor.
10. You shall not desire your neighbor's wife, his house, his field, his servants, his ox, his donkey, or anything that he owns.

The Shema

Moshe recites the *Shema*: "Hear Israel, God is our God, God is One."

This is followed by the command to love God "with all your heart, with all your soul, and with all your wealth." Each person must teach the commandments to his children and keep the commandments day and night, wherever they go.

Finally, Moshe tells B'nai Yisrael to put the Shema in their tefillin, and in their mezuzot.

Forgetting God

Moshe points out what will happen when B'nai Yisrael build up the Land of Israel. Things will be good, and their cities and houses will be filled with wonderful food. But they will forget that they did not build their houses and orchards by themselves — God gave them everything.

"Beware," Moshe exhorts them, "that you do not forget God and follow after gods of others. Otherwise, God's jealousy will destroy you.

"Instead, you should do what is fair and good in the eyes of God, so that it will be well with you, and you will inherit the good Land that God promised your forefathers."

Teaching Your Children

Then Moshe tells the people, "If your child asks you, 'What are the laws that God commanded you?' Answer by saying, 'We were slaves in Egypt, and God took us out with a mighty Hand. God brought us to the Land He swore to our forefathers. And God commanded us to obey the statutes, and to fear God, so it will be good with us all the days of our lives.'"

The Seven Nations

Moshe tells B'nai Yisrael that, although the seven nations who live in the Land of Israel are stronger than them, they will be no match for them.

But when B'nai Yisrael conquer these nations, Moshe warns the people in God's name, "Do not intermarry with these nations; do not give your daughter to their son, nor take their daughter for your son. If you do, then your child will turn away from Me and worship the gods of others.

"For you are a holy people to God," Moshe concludes, "And God has chosen you from among all the other nations of the world. Not because you are more numerous than other nations, but because He loves you and He keeps the oath He swore to your forefathers. That's why He took you out of Egypt."

THE HAFTARAH CONNECTION

(Yeshayahu 40:1-26)

This is the first of the seven "prophecies of comfort" read between the Fast of the Ninth of Av and Rosh Hashana.

Our Haftarah begins with the words, "You should be comforted, you should be comforted my nation." It talks of the bright future for which B'nai Yisrael are destined.

FOOD FOR THOUGHT

1) The commandment not to subtract anything from God's laws is understood, but why are we also prohibited from adding to them?

2) There are subtle differences between the Ten Commandments as explained in our Parsha and the way they are explained in Shemot 20:1-20. What do you think these differences come to tell us?

3) Which is better, to love God or to be in awe of him. Why?

4) Moshe tells the nation not to test God like they tested him in Masa. How did B'nai Yisrael test God there? See Shemot 17:1-7.

5) Why do you think the Shema, sometimes referred to as "the martyr's prayer," plays such a central role in Judaism? What are elements of belief that make up this verse?

TABLE TALK
DVAR TORAH

The beginning of the Parsha tells us of the great effort Moshe made in order to receive permission to enter the holy Land of Israel.

The Midrash tells us that Moshe drew a circle around himself, donned sackcloth, and told God that he wasn't going to leave the circle unless God revoked his decree and let him go into the promised Land.

Why was it so important for Moshe to be able to set foot in Israel?

One possibility is that Moshe, during the last days of his life, wanted to be able to fulfill as many commandments as possible. We all know that there are certain commandments that can only be kept in Israel, like Teruma – giving a percentage of your produce to the Kohen, and Shmitta – the seventh year Sabbatical of the Land. Moshe knew that unless he entered the Land, he would die without having performed all the mitzvot.

The Midrash also tells us that when Moshe realized he would not be able to set foot in the Land, he asked God to turn him into a bird, so that he could at least fly over the Land. If his concern was to keep the commandments, what good was it to be a bird?

Clearly, Moshe felt that even the very air of Israel was special. As our Rabbis say, "The air of Israel makes one wise."

Moshe wanted to soar over the Land because there is a holiness to the Land of Israel that permeates even the air above it.

It is no secret that each country has its own unique quality; it's own special flavor for which it is known. When it comes to foods, France has wine, Italy has pasta, America has fast food. But Israel has a special flavor reminiscent of the mahn in the desert, a flavor given to it by God. Israel has the flavor of holiness.

Moshe understood what generations of Jews have learned over the centuries, namely, that there is a special relationship between the people of Israel, the God of Israel, and the Land of Israel.

Nowhere is this more evident than in the survival of the State of Israel, a survival that goes beyond guns and bullets, beyond diplomacy and alliances. The State of Israel is living proof that God watches His Land and His People, and protects them from their enemies.

Moshe would have done anything to fly over the Land of Israel, to feel its holiness. How fortunate are we to be able to fly to the Land of Israel and partake of its unique flavor.

WISDOM OF THE SAGES

Va'et'hanan is always read on the Shabbat after the Fast of the Ninth of Av. Rabbi Yisrael of Koznitch explains the reason behind this.

The Ninth of Av is the only day Jews are not permitted to study Torah. The reason for this is that it's a sad day and learning Torah makes one happy. We read Va'et'hanan after the Fast because it contains the Ten Commandments which symbolize the fact that once again we may resume learning Torah.

"And God became angry at me, for you." (3:26)

What does Moshe mean when he says "for you?" Doesn't he mean "because of you"?

Moshe realized that the nation needed a new leader, one who could understand the "new generation." Moshe was saying, that while God became angry at me and wouldn't let me into the Land, things worked out well for you, because you received a new leader.

"And love your God...with all your heart." (6:5)

Rashi explains that it means to love God with both the *Yetzer Tov,* "the good inclination," and the *Yetzer Ha'ra,* "the evil inclination."

How can one love God with the evil inclination?

When we can admit that we have sinned because of the evil inclination, and we don't try to justify our evil actions, then we love God through our evil inclinations.

TELL IT WITH A SMILE *Moshe was not the only one who desired to be in Israel after he died.*

A woman enters an El Al plane carrying a small piece of luggage. When questioned, she explains that she has her dog Fifi in the luggage and wants to buy Fifi an extra ticket.

The steward tells her that no dogs are allowed on the plane, but there is a special compartment for them with the luggage. After arguing with the agent, the woman finally gives in.

When the plane arrives at Ben Gurion Airport in Israel, the steward is shocked to find out that the dog is dead. He quickly summons his assistant and has him buy the exact same dog from a pet shop not too far from the airport.

The woman takes one look at the dog and starts screaming frantically, "That's not my dog!"

"Of course, it's your dog," insists the steward.

"It's not! It's not!" she screams.

"How do you know?" asks the steward.

"Because my dog is dead! I was bringing him here to be buried in the Holy Land."

GEMMATRIA

Va'et'hanan... (3:23), "And I pleaded....

Moshe tells B'nai Yisrael that he pleaded with God for them. The Da'at Zekainim tells us that Moshe actually recited 515 prayers for B'nai Yisrael. This is hinted to in the numeric value of the word *Va'et'hanan,* which has a numeric value of 515!

עקב

THIS WEEK IN THE PARSHA

The Rewards of Keeping the Commandments

Moshe tells the people that in return for observing the laws of the Torah, God will safeguard them and deal kindly with them. God will bless them with abundance, and they will conquer all their enemies in the Land of Israel. But the conquest will not occur all at once. Rather, God will help B'nai Yisrael destroy their enemies little by little, so that the wild beasts will not overrun the Land.

The Miracles of the Desert

Moshe reminds the people about the miracles that were done for them in the desert. God gave them mahn so that they would know that "man does not live by bread alone." God also made sure that their clothes did not wear out and that their feet did not swell.

Therefore, when they arrive in the bountiful Land of Israel, eat their fill and are satisfied, they must bless God for the good Land.

The Problem of Prosperity

Moshe warns the people that when they are in the Land and things are going well, they should not forget who is behind their prosperity.

B'nai Yisrael should not say in their hearts, "My strength and the power of my hand brought me all this wealth." Rather, they must remember that it was God who gave them the strength so that they could accumulate wealth.

Moshe Remembers the Golden Calf

"Remember, do not forget," Moshe tells B'nai Yisrael, "that you provoked God in the desert, from the day you left Egypt until your arrival here."

Moshe then recounts how he was on Mt. Sinai for 40 days and nights. He reminds the people that when he saw the Golden Calf he smashed the first Tablets, and that God wanted to destroy them all. God was even angry at Aaron for his role in the Golden Calf, and Moshe had to pray for his brother, as well as for the people.

"Then God told me to carve two Tablets like the first ones and go up the mountain," where God inscribed the Ten Commandments again. God also told Moshe to make a wooden Ark to store both the broken Tablets and the new Tablets.

What God Asks

"And now, Israel," Moshe informs the Children of Israel, "What does God ask of you? Only that you fear Him and go in His ways, and that you love Him and worship Him with all your heart and all your soul, observing His commandments and statutes which I command you, for your own good."

The Second Chapter of Shema

Since the Land of Israel is dependent on God for its rain, Moshe tells the people how to make certain that God gives them the rain they need.

"If you listen to My commandments," he says in the name of God, "to love God and serve Him with all your heart and soul, then I will send the rain in its proper time, the early and late rains.

"But if your heart turns you away and you worship other gods, then I will be angry and close up the heavens so that there will be no rain."

In order to make sure that God's words are brought home, the people are commanded to teach these words to their children and to "write them on the doorposts of your house and on your gates." (This is the commandment of Mezuza)

THE HAFTARAH CONNECTION

(Yeshayahu 49:14-51:3)

This is the second of the "seven prophecies of comfort," read between the Fast of the Ninth of Av and Rosh Ha'shana.

The prophet guarantees that a new and improved B'nai Yisrael will soon be united with the Land of Israel, and God will "turn her ruins into a paradise and her wilderness into a garden of God."

In our Parsha, we find the verse that serves as the source for reciting the *Shema* in the morning and evening. It serves to teach us the proper approach to learning Torah.

The verse says, "and you shall teach them to your children and speak of them when you are at home, when you are traveling, when you lie down, and when you wake up." (11:19)

There seems to be a contradiction between this verse and the one in the book of Yehoshua. There it says "And you shall study it (the Torah) day and night," implying 24 hours a day.

How can it be that Yehoshua is commanded to study it day and night, while the Torah sets aside specific times for studying the Torah?

Rabbi Zeharia Breuer explains that it appears as if the Torah never really expected us to be able to sit and learn for 24 hours a day, seven days a week, 365 days a year. There are other duties which are also important, such as working, helping friends and neighbors, etc.

However, the Torah expects us to fill our "free" time with Torah study. That is why the verse begins with the words "when you are at home." After coming home from work, God expects everyone to spend some time learning. We also have time to study when we travel on a plane or train and before we go to sleep. We can even wake up a few minutes earlier than usual to learn a little.

God expects us to utilize our time in order to enhance our Torah knowledge. Anyone who studies during those periods, has, in essence, fulfilled the commandment found in the book of Yehoshua, "And you shall study it day and night."

WISDOM OF THE SAGES

"And you will know with your heart that like a man who rebukes his son, so too, God rebukes you." (8:5)

Rabbi Shimshon Refael Hirsch asks why the verse uses the term *"with* your heart"*, as opposed to the more common term *"in* your heart?"

He explains that there is an important difference between the two. To know "in your heart" is to understand something by using your heart as an organ of perception or thought. However, to know "with your heart" is not just to understand, but to take that understanding with you in whatever you do. A Jew is meant to take the experiences of reward and punishment that God has given him and carry them forward throughout his life.

"Watch yourself so that you don't forget God..." (8:11)

This opening verse comes right after the verse telling us to eat, be satisfied, and bless God. Why is this?

A man is usually most likely to turn against God when he is satisfied. A person then feels that he has no need for God. It is at this stage that the Torah warns us to be careful.

"And cleave to Him." (11:22)

How can we possibly "cleave" to God? After all, we know it's dangerous to get too close to God. The closer you get to God, the closer He watches you, and the more carefully you have to do the commandments of God.

Our Sages say that this means that you should cling to the leaders and wise men of each generation, and learn from them. If you do this, God perceives your actions as if you have clung to God Himself.

1) Everyone knows that Israel is a land "flowing with milk and honey." What else, according to the Parsha, is the Land blessed with?

2) Moshe tells B'nai Yisrael that "All God asks of you is that you hold Him in fear (awe), follow in His path, and serve Him." Why does Moshe make it appear like this is such a simple task?

3) How does the second chapter of Shema (11:13-21) follow logically from the first chapter (Devarim 6:4-9)?

God commands B'nai Yisrael not to be afraid of their enemies.

The threat of war was very serious, and the instructor at the military academy was preparing the future soldiers for combat.

He pointed to Goldberg and said, "Now then, private, suppose you're alone in the jungle, and suddenly the enemy jumps out of a tree and comes at you with a three foot knife. What steps will you take?"

"Very big ones," answered the private. "Backwards!"

GEMMATRIA V'haysear Ha'Shem mimha kol choly, "And God will remove all illness from you." (7:15)

The words *kol choly*, "all illness," have the numeric value of 98. God is telling B'nai Yisrael that if they listen to Him, He will remove all the 98 curses which could befall B'nai Yisrael, and which are mentioned in the Parsha of Ke Tavo.

ראה

Bringing Offerings

Moshe tells B'nai Yisrael that they are to bring their offerings to the place that God will show them. They cannot bring their offerings to just anyplace they want to.

Eating Meat

"When you want to eat meat," and Moshe assures them, you will have such a desire, "you may eat to your heart's content."

If a person lives far from the place that God designates for bringing offerings, then he is permitted to slaughter his animals and eat the meat in the cities. A person can eat meat whether he is pure or not pure.

However, Moshe warns, "Be strong – don't eat the blood – for the blood is the life, and you cannot eat the life with the meat. You must pour the blood on the ground like water."

The Commandments are Perfect

Moshe tells B'nai Yisrael that they have to do every mitzva that God commands, "Do not add to it nor subtract from it."

The False Prophet

If someone claims to be a prophet, Moshe warns, and he has dreams, and produces signs or miracles, all the while telling you to follow other gods, do not listen to him. "God is testing you to know whether you love Him with all your heart and all your soul."

The penalty for being a false prophet, Moshe tells them, is death. It is important that "you destroy the evil from among you."

Tempting Others

Moshe tells B'nai Yisrael that if a family member, a wife, or a friend says, "Let's go and worship the gods of others," don't listen. That person must be killed. Don't have pity on such a person. Everyone should take note of what happens to someone like this and learn not to do such a terrible thing.

The Perverse City

Moshe now describes the *Ir ha'nedahat,* the perverse city.

If the inhabitants of one of the cities of B'nai Yisrael are leading people astray by saying, "Let's go and worship the gods of others," then the city, with everything in it, must be burned.

Following Alien Customs

Moshe warns the people that, since they are children of God, they cannot follow the practices of those nations that mourn their dead by cutting themselves and tearing out their hair.

Kosher Animals

Moshe repeats some of the laws of kosher animals. Only kosher animals may be eaten by B'nai Yisrael.

1) Every animal that has split hooves, which are completely separated, and chews its cud, is kosher. However, the camel, the hare, the coney, and the pig have only one sign and are therefore not kosher.

2) Every fish that has fins and scales is kosher.

3) The clean birds can be eaten. However, there are many birds that are not clean.

4) Any animal that is not ritually slaughtered is not kosher. A Jew can give the carcass of an animal to the stranger in his city, or sell it to the non-Jew.

5) A Jew may not cook meat in milk.

Additional Ma'aser

Moses explains the laws of yearly *ma'aser*, called tithing. The people must take a portion of their produce as well as the firstborn of their cattle and flocks to the place that God chooses. Only there may they eat them.

If the place that God chooses is too far from where a person lives, he can exchange the ma'aser for money. When he gets to this special place, he is to spend the money there.

At the end of three years, a portion of his crops have to be brought to the cities to be given to the Levite, the convert, the orphan and the widow who are in the cities.

Shmitta

Moshe explains that at the end of seven years there is the law of Shmitta. All loans are to be cancelled. The reward for doing this is that there will be no poor among the people and that God will bless the Land.

Furthermore, even if the Shmitta year is approaching, it is important for one Jew to help out another. Therefore, Moshe tells them, if a poor person needs a loan, you must give it with an open heart.

The Slave

Moshe tells the people that if a Jew becomes so poor that he must be sold into slavery, that Jew can only be a slave to another Jew for six years. On the seventh year, he is to be set free. When he leaves his master, he should be sent out with animals from his master's flocks, and wine. After all, B'nai Yisrael must remember they were slaves in Egypt, and God took them out.

But if the slave does not want to leave his master, the master must take an awl and put it through the slave's ear, into the door. He will be a slave to the master forever.

The Three Major Festivals

Moshe describes the three major pilgrimage festivals to B'nai Yisrael.

❖**PESAH:** This holiday must be celebrated in the spring because God took the Jewish people out of Egypt in the springtime. The sacrifices of this holiday include sheep and cattle. But no leavened bread can be eaten with the sacrifice. For seven days only matza may be eaten, because it is the bread of affliction and B'nai Yisrael left Egypt in haste.

The Pesah sacrifice can only be done in the place

that God shows the people. The sacrifice is to be roasted on an open fire.

❖**SHAVUOT:** B'nai Yisrael are told to count seven weeks from when the sickle cuts the crop. Then the people are to celebrate Shavuot. They are to give voluntary offerings to God, as much as they wish, in accordance with what God has given them. Once again, they must remember that they were slaves in Egypt.

Everyone is to rejoice in the place that God appoints.

❖**SUKKOT:** This is a seven-day festival that coincides with the gathering and threshing of the produce, including wine.

Here too, the celebration is to take place where God tells them.

The people must appear before God during these three festivals. No one is to come empty-handed; everyone is to bring what he can, according to what God has given him.

THE HAFTARAH CONNECTION

(Yeshayahu 54:11-55:5)

This is the third of the seven "prophecies of comfort," read between the Fast of the Ninth of Av and Rosh Hashana.

In this Haftarah, God comforts the nation by telling them what benefits those who follow God's path will reap.

He says that B'nai Yisrael's moral influence in the world will be so great that nations whom B'nai Yisrael have never even heard of will come flocking to them.

TABLE TALK
DVAR TORAH

In our Parsha we find explicit permission to eat the flesh of an animal, but a strong prohibition against eating any of the blood (12:23). This limitation seems a bit strange. Why can't we eat all of the animal?

The Rambam, in his book, "The Guide For The Perplexed," gives the following explanation.

It is necessary for the Torah to set limitations when it comes to eating the flesh of an animal because killing – even for food – is a serious act. We can't just slaughter animals as the mood moves us, without rules and regulations. It is these rules and regulations that serve to create a sensitivity and understanding which we must apply into our relationship with the animal kingdom.

This, however, doesn't explain why the blood of a kosher animal was singled out as the only thing which we must refrain from consuming.

Rabbi Shimshon Refael Hirsch bases his answer to this question on our Parsha. It says in 12:23 that "The blood is the life." The blood of any creature flows through the entire body, giving the animal life and vitality. The blood is therefore called the life. And the blood of an animal, which is grounded in purely physical needs, should not mix with the blood – the nature, the soul – of a human being which is holy and capable of lofty ideals. The lifeblood of an animal would surely taint the "life" of man.

So the Torah uses the words "Be strong" to urge us to overcome our desire for blood.

Rabbi Shimon ben Azai learns yet another principle for the words "Be strong." These words come to teach us not only to keep away from eating blood but also how we should relate to the commandments. For if we must be strong not to eat blood, which is certainly a simple enough commandment to keep, how much more so must we muster up our strength and be especially strong when it comes to fulfilling the more difficult commandments in the Torah.

WISDOM OF THE SAGES

"And you shall eat there before God, and rejoice in all you have." (12:7)

This instruction in how to serve God is a very important element in Judaism. In many other religions, man's service to his god is expressed through a deprivation of physical pleasures. Our God prefers that we enjoy the many beautiful things given to us by Him, while making sure to raise this enjoyment to a level of service to God.

"And you shall rejoice before God, you, your children, your servants..." (12:12)

Why must this happiness take on a communal form. Isn't it enough that each person feels happy by himself?

Not at all. A person is required to share his happiness with those he loves and those less fortunate than himself. Sharing adds yet another, greater dimension to one's happiness.

"You shall open your hand wide to him." (15:8)

Here we are commanded to give handsomely to the poor. Why is it that before we give charity, which is such an important commandment, we don't have to recite a blessing?

One reason is to make us understand that a person is not an object. Before we bite into an apple we thank God for giving us the opportunity to make a blessing on this food. But a person is someone with feelings. If there was a blessing made over giving charity, *tzedaka,* it would greatly offend the poor people. They would think that the only reason you're giving them anything is to be able to make another blessing.

1) Moshe tells the nation that they will bring the offerings to "The place that God chooses as His resting place" (12:11). We know that this place is Jerusalem. But why doesn't God name this resting place?

2) A city that's destroyed because its inhabitants worshipped idols cannot be rebuilt. Why not?

3) Why do you think that God wants B'nai Yisrael to come to Jerusalem three times a year? What is so special about the three times mentioned in our Parsha?

TELL IT WITH A SMILE

There are certain things that we aren't allowed to eat, but sometimes just being allowed to eat something doesn't make it edible.

Shmulik decided to go out with a bunch of friends to a restaurant on the far side of town.

He ordered the "special," but it was terrible. The meat was as tough as leather, the mashed potatoes looked and tasted like glue, and the peas were like pellets.

"Waiter," he yelled, "this meal is disgusting. Call the manager!"

190

"It won't do you a bit of good," replied the waiter. "He won't eat it either!"

GEMMATRIA **Banim atem La'Shem...** "You are all children of God..." (14:1)

If you count up the words in the verse, you will find that there are 12 words. This is coming to tell us that all 12 tribes are of equal importance before God. We are all His children.

שופטים

The Courts

Moshe tells the people to appoint judges and officers for the tribes. They have to judge with righteousness so that the people will possess the Land that God gives them.

The people are then warned not to plant an idolatrous Asherah tree or erect a pillar for idol worship near the Altar of God.

The Penalty for Idol Worship

Moshe cautions B'nai Yisrael that the penalty for idol worship is stoning. But there must be two witnesses or three witnesses to condemn the person to death; a single witness is not enough.

The High Court

If people in the cities have a dispute about matters which the local courts cannot settle, then they should go to the place where God chooses. There the Kohanim, Levites, and the judge of the day will determine the outcome.

Moshe tells the people, "You must do as the judges say and be careful to do as they teach you. Do not deviate from what they tell you, neither to the right nor the left."

If someone maliciously decides not to listen to what the Kohen or the judge says, that person shall die.

The King

Moshe says that the time will come when B'nai Yisrael will ask for a king "like all the nations that are around." The king they choose must be a Jew. He may not own too many horses, or he may be tempted to take the people back to Egypt. He may not have too many wives because they may lead him astray. Nor may he own too much silver and gold.

The king must write two copies of the Torah. One copy must be with him and he should read from it always, so that he does not become arrogant nor deviate from the commandments.

Prophecy

Now Moshe lists the kinds of false prophets and soothsayers that exist among the other nations: sorcerers, astrologers, and animal charmers, among others. The other nations have only these to listen to, but B'nai Yisrael have God.

When a prophet arises among the people, who speaks in the Name of God, and declares that certain things will happen, but never do, then he is a false prophet.

Cities of Refuge

Moshe reminds the people that a person who kills unintentionally can go to a city of refuge. Three such cities are to be established on the eastern side of the Jordan River and three on the western side of the Jordan, after B'nai Yisrael enter the Land.

God does not want innocent blood to be shed in the Land by

the families who will avenge the murdered person. That is why He has set aside these cities of refuge.

Moving Boundaries

Moshe tells the people that it is forbidden to move a boundary between your property and that of your neighbor's without his consent. God has designated the boundaries of each person.

False Witnesses

Moshe now discusses the laws of witnesses.

A single witness cannot give testimony against someone who has sinned. Only two witnesses or three witnesses can testify to such matters.

If there are false witnesses then the judge should do to the witnesses what they wanted to do to the accused.

B'nai Yisrael at War

Moshe explains the rules of war to B'nai Yisrael.

"When you go out to battle against your enemy, do not fear them, for God is with you. When you draw near to the battle, the Kohen should speak to the people saying, 'Do not be afraid or panic, for God goes with you.' "

Then the officers are to announce who is exempt from going to war:

℘ Anyone who has built a new house and not lived in it.

℘ Anyone who has planted a vineyard and not eaten from it.

℘ Anyone who is betrothed to a woman and has not lived with her.

℘ Anyone who is faint-hearted.

The reason for the first three exemptions is that someone else will benefit from what the person began. The reason for the fourth exemption is that a person who is afraid may make others afraid as well.

Next, Moshe explains that when the people come to a city, they must first call out for peace. If the other nation refuses to make peace, then B'nai Yisrael are to kill all the males and take everything else as booty.

"But of the nations that God gives you as an inheritance — the Hiti, Emori, Canaani, Prizi, Hivi, Yevusi — no one in their cities is to be left alive. This is so you won't learn to worship their gods and be like them."

Finally, Moshe tells the people that when they lay siege to a city, they are not permitted to cut down the fruit trees. However, they can use non-fruit-bearing trees to make armaments against the city.

The Calf of Atonement

Moshe tells the people the law of *Eglah Arufah*.

If a corpse is found in the field, the elders and judges should measure the distance between the corpse and the surrounding cities. The elders of the city nearest the corpse must take a calf which has never been used for work, bring it to a stream, and kill it by cutting its neck in the stream.

The Kohanim should approach. Then the elders of the city wash their hands over the calf and say, "Our hands have not spilled the blood of this person, nor did we see who did it." They then ask God to take the blood of the calf as an atonement.

Of course, the people still have to hunt for the murderer.

TABLE TALK
DVAR TORAH

Our Parsha describes the different segments of the population that will exist when the Jewish people enter the Land. One of the subjects addressed by the Torah within this context is the uniqueness of the Tribe of Levi.

The Torah, in the first verse of chapter 18, states that the Tribe of Levi will not receive a portion of the Land when B'nai Yisrael enter Israel. Therefore, they will eat from the offerings brought in the Temple. The very next verse repeats this message. Again we read that the Tribe of Levi won't receive a portion of the Land, for God is their inheritance.

Why did the Torah have to repeat that the Tribe of Levi has no inheritance in the Land of Israel?

In order to resolve the problem, it is important to understand the value of owning a piece of land, and what the Tribe of Levi received instead of Land.

When B'nai Yisrael entered the Land, land itself had great significance. In the agricultural society that existed then, those who had no land, had nothing to eat! Therefore, it stands to reason that if the Levites were to survive, they would need food. This food came as a tithe on all agricultural foods produced by the other 11 tribes.

Nevertheless, despite this compensation, which provides for the physical welfare of the Levites, there is still something missing. They have no place to call home.

God has a solution for this as well: "God is their inheritance" (18:2). What does that mean? It tells us that God's home is their home. The place they can call home is none other than the Temple itself!

We can now understand why the Torah tells us twice that the Tribe of Levi will have no inheritance in the Land. The first time it is to show us that the Levites get tithes from all the other tribes, and the second time teaches us that indeed "there is no place like home," God's home.

THE HAFTARAH CONNECTION

(Yeshayahu 51:12-52:12)

This is the fourth of the "seven prophecies of comfort" read between the Fast of the Ninth of Av and Rosh Hashana.

Our Haftarah begins with God saying: "I am the one who comforts you."

God assures us that we will soon be redeemed, and we will make our way back to Israel.

With a promise like that from God, we have no reason to be afraid of any nation.

FOOD FOR THOUGHT

1) If someone worships idols and is convicted by the court, he is killed by stoning. The Torah tells us that the two witnesses who brought about his conviction become the executioners. Why is it so important that they receive this task?

2) The Torah lists three limitations to the king's absolute power – horses, wives, and wealth – but gives us only the reason for limiting the number of horses and wives a king may own. What do you think the reasons for the other limitation might be?

3) The army, even during a time of war, must keep to a high moral standard. How do we see this from our Parsha?

GEMMATRIA *Ke tavo el ha'aretz...* "When you enter the land.." (17:14)

Moshe tells B'nai Yisrael that when they enter the Land they will want to appoint a king. The numeric value of the words *Ki tavo,* "when you enter," is 439. This is the same value as the words *Bemay Shmuel,* "In the days of Shmuel." It was during the days of Shmuel that B'nai Yisrael asked him to appoint a king for them.

WISDOM OF THE SAGES **"And if the Levi shall come from one of your gates..."** (18:6)

But isn't this whole passage referring to the Kohanim and not to the Levites?

Rabbi Shimshon Refael Hirsch explains why the Kohanim are referred to as Levites. In the desert, the Kohanim served in the Mishkan and lived in tents around it. In Israel, however, the Kohanim lived where they chose, coming to work in Jerusalem only when it was their respective shift. This allowed them plenty of time to help out the Levites in their job as teachers of the Torah. That is why they too are known as Levites.

There was a special Kohen known as "the Kohen anointed for battle" whose function was to give the nation a pep talk before going out to fight. He would tell all those who were going to fight not to lose heart, but to trust in God. The Tractate in Sota 42a explains why this passage comes right after the passage dealing with justice and honesty. It is to teach us that if we deal fairly with one another, then we will never lose heart and will therefore never need to fear hostile enemies.

❖

"...you shall not destroy its trees." (20:19)

When setting siege to a city, we are prohibited from destroying the fruit-bearing trees in the process. It is from this verse that our Sages learn the law of *Ba'al Tash'hit*, the prohibition against wasting anything that can be used.

Perhaps that is why parents have always told their children not to waste food during supper!

TELL IT WITH A *Sometimes judges are faced with really difficult decisions.*

SMILE The defendant was a second offender being sentenced by the judge for robbing a house.

"For stealing during the day, I am fining you 10,000 dollars and sentencing you to six months community service," said the judge.

"What!" exclaimed the criminal. "Last year you gave me a fine for stealing at night, and now you fine me for stealing during the day.

"Tell me, your honor, just when do you expect me to make my living?"

כִּי תֵצֵא

THIS WEEK IN THE PARSHA

The Captive Woman

If, during a war, a soldier sees a beautiful woman, captures her and takes her home, he must shave her head and let her nails grow. She must change the clothes she wore and mourn her parents for a month. Then he can marry her.

But if he decides he doesn't want to marry her, then he has to let her go. He cannot sell her or enslave her, because he has humbled her.

The Firstborn's Rights

If a man has two wives, one whom he loves and one whom he hates, and his firstborn is from his hated wife, he must nevertheless give a double portion of his inheritance to the firstborn.

The Rebellious Son

If a man has a rebellious son who won't listen to his parents no matter what they do, then his parents have to take him to the elders of the city and declare: "This son of ours is rebellious. He does not listen to us. He is a glutton and a drunkard."

Then the boy is to be put to death by stoning.

Hanging A Murderer

If someone commits a murder and is put to death, his body is to be hung on a gallows. But his body must be buried on the same day. For a hanged person is an expression of God's curse, and such a sight would profane the Land.

Property of Others

If you see a lost animal, don't ignore it. Return the animal to its owner or, if you don't know who the owner is, bring it to your house. When the owner searches for it, you will then be able to return the animal. This also holds true for any lost article.

If a donkey or ox is falling down because of its load, you must help the owner pick up the animal.

Cross Dressing

Men's clothes should not be worn by women, and women's clothes should not be worn by men.

The Bird's Nest

If you come upon a bird's nest and want the eggs or the young, you must send away the mother bird before taking them. This act will prolong your days.

Kelayim

You may not sow your vineyard with two different species. This is called *Kelayim*. Nor may you plow with an ox and donkey tied together.

Shatnes

You may not wear wool and linen combined together. This is called Shatnes.

A Wife Defamed

Note: A betrothed woman is a married woman who has not yet lived with her husband.

If a man claims that his wife was not a virgin when she was bethrothed, then the parents of the woman must bring proof of her virginity to the elders of the city.

If it turns out that the husband has defamed his wife, he is fined 100 shekels which he must give to his wife's father. Furthermore, he can never divorce his wife.

If the accusation is true, then she is put to death by stoning, because she had committed adultery.

The Married Woman

If a man has intimate relations with another man's wife, they are both put to death.

The Betrothed Woman

Note: A betrothed woman is a married woman who has not yet lived with her husband.

If a man meets a betrothed woman in the city and has intimate relations with her, they are both put to death by stoning. The woman is killed, because she did not cry out for help. The man is killed, because he raped her.

But if a man meets a betrothed woman in the field and rapes

out the memory of Amalek from under the heavens. Don't forget."

Additional Laws in the Parsha

1. If you build a new house you must make a fence around the roof so no one will fall off.

2. You should make twisted threads on the four corners of your garment. This is called *Tzitzit.*

3. A *mamzer* is a child born from incest or adultery. Such a child cannot marry into the nation.

4. An Ammonite or Moabite cannot marry into the Jewish nation. The descendants of an Edomite or Egyptian who convert may marry into the nation after the third generation.

5. You cannot turn in an escaped slave. He can live wherever he chooses among the Jewish people. No one is permitted to taunt him.

6. Male or female prostitutes should not be found in the nation.

7. A Jew is not to cause another Jew to take interest. However, a Jew may cause a non-Jew to take interest.

8. You must carry out any vow to God that you make.

9. If you are a laborer, you may eat as much grapes or grain as you wish in the fields of another. But you cannot take the food away with you.

10. A man does not go into the army during his first year of marriage.

11. A man who kidnaps another man, enslaving him and selling him, is to be killed.

12. When you hire someone, you must pay him that day.

13. A person who is found guilty and whose penalty is lashes cannot receive no more than 40 lashes.

14. Don't muzzle your ox on the threshing floor.

15. You must have honest weights and measures.

 **1) The reward for sending away the mother bird before taking its eggs is long life. The same reward is received for honoring one's parents. Why do you think these two commandments have the same reward?**

2) We are not allowed to loathe an Egyptian, even though the Egyptians enslaved us, because we were strangers in their land. What should we learn from this about how to treat strangers?

3) Why can't we put a muzzle on an animal while it's working in the field?

THE HAFTARAH CONNECTION

(Yeshayahu 54:1-10)

This is the fifth of the seven "prophecies of comfort" read between the Fast of the Ninth of Av and Rosh Hashana.

One of the keys to a nation's survival is its numbers. Being fruitful is one of the best blessings a people can receive.

In our Haftarah, God comforts the Jewish people by promising that all their barren women will give birth and that their desolate cities will be inhabited.

TABLE TALK
DVAR TORAH

At the end of the Parsha, we come across one of the most electrifying commandments in the Torah, the command to totally destroy any and all trace of the nation known as Amalek.

When we think of this mitzva, a question immediately comes to mind: What did this nation do to deserve total annihilation? There were plenty of other nations that fought with B'nai Yisrael in the desert, and God did not single them out for such total destruction.

Let's first understand: Who were the people of Amalek?

They were nomads. They did not have any land they called their own. They wandered from place to place, making their living by stealing from innocent wayfarers.

Why did Amalek attack B'nai Yisrael?

That is harder to understand. We know that the other nations that attacked B'nai Yisrael did it out of fear, or because they felt threatened by this new nation. We read how the Edomites and Amorites attacked when B'nai Yisrael came too close to their borders. As reasons go, the other nations had good reason to fight B'nai Yisrael.

But what motivated Amalek to attack the fledgling Jewish nation? The people of Amalek had no land for the Jewish nation to threaten. And B'nai Yisrael, for their part, stayed clear of all the nomadic tribes. They were not looking for trouble.

So, what prompted Amalek to be the first to attack the Jewish people?

Our Sages compare what Amalek did to the case of a boiling body of water which everyone is afraid to jump into. One fool jumps into the water. Even though he is scalded, by jumping in he brings down the temperature of the water, making it easier for others to follow his lead.

Amalek knew of the miracles that God had performed for His people, but they didn't care. They wanted to show the rest of the world that B'nai Yisrael were not invincible, even if it resulted in their — Amalek's — destruction.

For this reason, the Amalek people began their attack, not against the army of B'nai Yisrael, but against the old and weary who trailed behind the main body of the Jewish people. That's why, when describing the attack, God says, "They cut off all those lagging to your rear."

Amalek never thought they could win the war. Their whole intent was just to prove to the world that it is possible to fight the Jews and hurt them, make them bleed.

A nation who harbors this sort of senseless hatred against B'nai Yisrael; a nation whose sole purpose is to demean and debase the God of the Jews, deserves no less than the pledge by God, and His people, to wipe it out, utterly and for all time.

WISDOM OF THE SAGES

"When you go out to wage war against your enemy." (21:10)

Here the Torah is giving us some sound military tactics, somewhat reminiscent of the saying, "The best defense is a good offense."

The Torah tells us that when waging war, it is best to "go out" and fight on the enemy's soil rather than on your own land.

"When you reap your harvest and forget a sheaf, you must not go back to get it, but leave it for the orphan..." (24:19)

This commandment has a unique element not found in other commandments. Every other commandment depends on our conscious intention to do the mitzva, whereas this commandment can only be fulfilled if a person forgets!

The Me'am Loez says that if God blesses a person for performing a mitzva unintentionally, by forgetting, how much more so is one blessed when he performs a mitzva intentionally.

"You shall not give him more than 40 lashes." (25:3)

The Torah says 40, yet we know that the maximum number of lashes one can get is only 39. Why not all 40?

Perhaps if the culprit received all 40 lashes he might think that since his punishment is complete, he doesn't have to repent. That's why the Sages said that he can get only 39 lashes. This way he knows that he hasn't been completely punished, and he will repent.

Nowadays we may not have such a thing as a "rebellious son," but we definitely have our share of troublemakers.

A famous Rabbi was taking an evening walk down the street, when he came upon little Joshua standing on tiptoe, trying to reach the doorbell.

"Hello Joshua," greeted the Rabbi. "Let me help you."

The boy waited until the Rabbi had pushed the buzzer, and then shouted, "Thanks Rabbi. Now run as fast as you can!"

GEMMATRIA The numeric value of the word *Amalek* is 240. This is the same numeric value as the Hebrew word *safek*, "doubt." The people of Amalek fought with B'nai Yisrael only because they didn't believe in God; they *doubted* His existence.

כי תבוא

Bringing First Fruits

When the people settle the Land of Israel they are to take the first fruits of their fields, put them in baskets and go to the place that God designates.

Each person is to go to the Kohen and declare that he has come to the Land that God promised his forefathers. The Kohen will then take the basket and place it in front of the Altar of God.

The person is to say, "An Arami tried to destroy my father. My father went down to Egypt and lived there, few in number, and then became a great nation. The Egyptians persecuted us and made us work hard. We called to God, and He listened and saw our suffering. God took us out of Egypt with a strong hand, with miracles and signs. He brought us to this place and gave us this Land flowing with milk and honey. And I have brought my first fruits to you, God."

The person bringing the fruits should be happy with all the good God has given him.

Confession of the Ma'aser

In the third year, when a person takes the *ma'aser* for the Levi, the convert, the orphan, and the widow, he has to declare that he has done the tithing according to the laws of God.

Crossing the Jordan River

Moshe tells the people that when they cross the Jordan River they are to set up stones and coat them with plaster. They must inscribe the Torah on these stones. These stones are to be set up on Mount Eval. Then an altar of uncut stones is to be set up and Peace Offerings are to be sacrificed on it.

Blessings and Curses

Moshe tells the tribes that, when they cross the Jordan they are to take positions on two mountains, Mt. Gerizim and Mt. Eval.

The tribes of Shimon, Levi, Yehuda, Yesahar, Yosef, and Binyamin are to stand on Mt. Gerizim. The tribes of Reuven, Gad, Asher, Zevulun, Dan, and Naftali are to stand on Mt. Eval.

The Levites will address the people in a loud voice saying:

> Cursed is the man who makes an idol and puts it in a secret place.
> Cursed is the person who holds his parents in low esteem.
> Cursed is the person who moves another's boundary.
> Cursed is the person who perverts judgment of a convert, orphan, or widow.
> Cursed is the person who lies with the wife of his father.
> Cursed is the person who lies with an animal.
> Cursed is the person who lies with his sister.
> Cursed is the person who lies with his mother-in-law.
> Cursed is the person who strikes another in secret.
> Cursed is the person who takes a bribe to kill an

innocent individual.

Cursed is the person who will not uphold the words
of this Torah, to perform them.

After each curse, the people are to say, "Amen!"
Moshe then tells the people the blessings which will come to
them if they observe the Torah:

You will be blessed in the city and in the field.
You will be blessed with children, your animals with
offspring, and your fields with produce.
You will be blessed when you come into your house
and when you go out.
God will destroy your enemies.
God will bless everything you do.
God will establish you as a holy nation because you
follow in His ways.
God will bring the rains in their time. You will lend to
other nations, but not have to borrow from anyone.
You will be the head of all nations, and not the tail.

Finally, Moshe enumerates, in great detail, the curses that
God will place on the Jewish people if they forsake Him. These
curses include:

God will send plagues.
God will send drought and famine.
God will send your enemy to destroy you.
Your sons and daughters will be given to others and
you will be powerless to do anything about it.
You will go mad with the sights that you see.
You will be scattered among the peoples of the world,
and you will know no peace.

Moshe Gives A Summary

Moshe calls all B'nai Yisrael and reminds them that they were witnesses to the miracles that God performed in Egypt. "But God did not give you a heart to know, or eyes to see, or ears to hear until today," Moshe adds.

He recalls the fact that their clothes did not wear away and their shoes did not wear out despite 40 years of wandering in the desert. He recounts the battles of Sihon and Og, and the distribution of their land among the tribes of Reuven, Gad, and half the tribe of Menashe.

If B'nai Yisrael observe the Torah, he tells them, they will be successful in all that they do.

THE HAFTARAH CONNECTION

(Yeshayahu 60:1-22)

This is the sixth of the seven "prophecies of comfort" read between the Fast of the Ninth of Av and Rosh Ha'shana.

Besides being a prophesy of comfort, this Haftarah is also connected to our Parsha.

One of the curses mentioned in our Parsha is that B'nai Yisrael have to either "shape up or ship out." God tells them that if they won't listen to Him, He will send them into exile by boat.

In our Haftarah, we find that the prophet mentions those same boats once again. Only this time, they serve the exact opposite purpose. God promises His people that, very soon, they will return from exile by boat.

Our Parsha begins by discussing the farmer's obligation to bring his first fruits to the Temple and to thank God for blessing his Land. The farmer is commanded to be full of joy and happiness as a result of all the plenty that God bestowed upon him.

Right after this, the Torah goes on to a different topic. It talks of the farmer's obligation to give a percentage of his crops to the poor, the orphans, and the widows, every third year.

What is the connection between the mitzva of joy and happiness to that of charity?

The Ba'al Ha'turim offers an explanation. He says that the connection between these two passages is that we can only be assured of happiness if we look after and provide for the needs of the poor and helpless.

There is no better example of the connection between happiness and charity than the holiday of Purim. During this holiday, we drink wine, prepare a special meal, and achieve the pinnacle of joy and happiness through dance and song. Yet, in the midst of all this celebration, we have a special mitzva of giving charity to the poor.

In Judaism, happiness and charity are linked in two ways:

First, we should feel good inside, but only when we know that those around us aren't suffering or hungry. How can a person feel content if his neighbor is starving?

Second, the blessing of joy and happiness which comes from God is only bestowed upon us when He sees that we are concerned with the welfare of others. When we can show concern for our fellow Jews, then God shows concern for us as well.

So we see that charity helps us to feel happy about ourselves, and ensures that God will grant us a special blessing of joy and contentment.

WISDOM
OF THE
SAGES

"And you shall rejoice in all the good that God gave you." (26:11)

If a person receives a beautiful gift from a king, he rejoices. This happiness may not come from the actual value of the gift, but from the fact that the gift came from the king himself.

The Torah is teaching us this same lesson. We must rejoice in everything that God gives us, even if we think the actual value of what we receive is not so great. When it comes from the King of Kings, that is cause enough for celebration.

"Look down from Your Holy place, and bless Your nation Israel." (26:15)

We say this statement after we bring *bikurim*, the first fruits, up to Jerusalem. What does this statement have to do with bikurim?

Rashi explains that we are telling God, "We have done our job of bringing the first fruits. Now God, You fulfill Your promise and bless us!"

"And it shall be on that day...you will set up big stones and write upon them all the words of this Torah." (27:2,3)

The Abarbanel comments that this verse highlights the difference between B'nai Yisrael and the other nations. When the other nations return victoriously from war, they commemorate their victory by establishing great monuments for themselves. The Jews, however, do not give tribute to themselves but rather to the Torah that they represent, and for which they fought.

In the midst of a physical victory, we acknowledge our faith by engraving the words of our Torah in stone!

 **1) When bringing the first fruits, why do we specifically mention the events of Lavan, Yaacov's father-in-law, and Egypt?**

2) Which, in your opinion, is the worst of all the possible curses that can befall B'nai Yisrael? Why?

3) Why is it that, if someone hits his friend in private, he is cursed? (27:24) Is it any worse than hitting a friend in public?

 *One of the curses in the Parsha is, "You will become crazy from what you see." Some people have a head-start on this curse.*

A Jew from Chelm visits Warsaw. In the main synagogue he hears the cantor ask a riddle: "Who is my father's son but not my brother?"

No one is able to answer.

"It's me," the cantor says.

The Chelm Jew is greatly impressed. He returns home and after prayers asks the congregation: "Who is my father's son but not my brother?"

No one knows.

"It's the cantor in Warsaw," he answers.

 One of God's names has the numeric value of 26 and is mentioned 26 times during *Shmoneh Esray,* the 18 blessings that form the core of Jewish prayer. This is done to counteract the 26 times that God's name is mentioned in the section of curses in the Parsha.

נצבים

The Eternal Covenant With God

Moshe gathers B'nai Yisrael together and declares that now the people are entering a covenant with God. This covenant binds both "those who are here today, and those who are not here today."

But, Moshe adds, if someone hearing this covenant feels that "Peace will be with me even though I do as I please," he should know that God will blot him out.

If, as time goes by, B'nai Yisrael do not keep the commandments the Land will no longer be able to grow anything. Other nations will ask, "Why did God do this to the Land?" The answer will be, "Because B'nai Yisrael left their covenant with God and went to serve idols. So God became angry with the Land and sent all the curses that are written in this Book, forcing the people out of the Land."

Then Moshe tells them that, "The hidden things are in God's hands, but the revealed things are for us and our children forever. We must carry out all the words of the Torah."

The Redemption

Moshe assures B'nai Yisrael that when they realize why they have been dispersed, they will fulfill the commandments with all their hearts and souls. Then God will have mercy on them and bring them back to their Land.

Where to Find the Torah

"The commandments that I command you today," Moshe explains, "are not hidden from you nor are they far from you. They are not in the heavens so that you can say, 'Who will go up to the heavens to get the commandments for us so we can hear them and do them?'

"And the commandments are not across the sea so that you can say, 'Who will cross the sea for us and get the commandments for us so we can hear them and do them?'

"Rather, what you seek is very close by. It can be done with your mouth and your heart."

The Choice

Moshe tells B'nai Yisrael that the choice of life and death is up to them. If you "walk in God's ways and observe His commandments, then you will live and multiply and God will bless you in the Land.

"But if your heart strays, and you do not listen, then you will surely be lost."

Finally, Moshe tells them "I call heaven and earth today to bear witness that I have placed life and death before you, blessing and curse. So choose life, so that you and your children will live."

The key to making the right choice is to love God and realize that He is your life.

TABLE TALK
DVAR TORAH

Our Parsha is one of the last times in which Moshe addresses B'nai Yisrael. The purpose of this final gathering is to prepare them for their entry into the Land of Israel.

The Parsha focuses on the *Brit*, "the covenant," between God and B'nai Yisrael. A covenant usually implies a situation in which both sides get together and decide on something that is mutually beneficial. That, however, isn't the case here. The covenant here is to be looked upon as a law. We, the Jews, don't get a say in the matter. Just like the "laws of nature" are forever set and unchangeable, so too this "spiritual law" which binds us to God forever, is set and unchangeable.

Throughout Jewish history, there have always been those who decide to turn their back on their heritage and ignore the covenant and all it entails. They feel that they can do whatever they want, however they want, whenever they want. Our Parsha compares these people to the fungus that is sometimes found on otherwise healthy roots. God promises that He will not forgive these people, and will bring upon them all the curses written in the previous Parsha.

But, when enough people deny their heritage, it can spread throughout the nation like a plague. Sometimes everyone becomes infected, and then God sends the entire nation out of the Land, into exile.

In so doing, God's intention is not so much to punish B'nai Yisrael as it is to correct their way of thinking. In this sense, B'nai Yisrael can be compared to a machine which has broken down. It must be sent back to the factory for repairs. So too, B'nai Yisrael, having sinned, are sent into exile for "repairs."

Exile is the best place for repairs, because there we feel the uniqueness of our nation. Whether we like it or not, we are constantly reminded of how different we are. This causes us to try and work to better ourselves, all the while striving to renew our bond and covenant with God.

Like the machine that is eventually fixed and returned to its owner, when we are fixed and realize our need to keep the covenant with God, we will be sent back home where we belong.

THE HAFTARAH CONNECTION

(Yeshayahu 61:10-63:9)

This is the last of the seven "prophecies of comfort" read between the Fast of the Ninth of Av and Rosh Ha'shana.

In our Haftarah, the prophet comforts the people and tells them that everyone will now know that B'nai Yisrael have not been forsaken. The walls of Jerusalem will be rebuilt, and God will no longer allow their crops to be taken away and eaten by other nations.

FOOD FOR THOUGHT

1) Moshe tells the nation that the covenant which is going to be made between B'nai Yisrael and God is going to bind future generations. How can that be?

2) Why did God appoint the heavens and earth as witnesses of the covenant?

GEMMATRIA

Atem nitzavim... "You are standing..." (29:9)

The numeric value of the word *Atem*, "You", is 441. This is the same numeric value as the word *Emet*, "truth."

From here we learn that B'nai Yisrael will be able to stand together only if they tell the truth.

WISDOM OF THE SAGES

"Your leaders, elders and policemen..." (29:9)

When Moshe called the people together why did he neglect to include "judges" in this list of distinguished people?

Judges are universally respected because they have the power to decide a person's guilt or innocence. Policemen, however, are usually in the role of the "bad guys," since they have the task of enforcing the judge's ruling. So, to make sure that the policemen received their fair share of honor, Moshe included the policemen instead of the judges.

❖

"For it is *very close to you*, in your mouth and in your heart, to do." (30:14)

The Talmud Nida 30b teaches us that a fetus is taught the entire Torah in his mother's womb. But, before he is born, an angel comes and causes him to forget it.

We learn from this that the Torah, which was once "in your mouth," once known to you, has now been forgotten. But it is always easier to remember something forgotten, than to have to learn it from scratch.

"For it is very close to you, *in your mouth and in your heart, to do.*" (30:14)

The mouth is mentioned before the heart, because sometimes, in order to get our hearts involved, we must first take action. That is why, even when we don't necessarily feel that we're "getting into it," we should not give up. Eventually our feelings will follow.

 *God says that the hidden things aren't for us to know. And even if we know, sometimes it's better not to tell others.*

Yossi Goldfarb, a poor immigrant silversmith, worked day and night so that he could give his son, Feivel, the best education possible. By the boy's 18th birthday, Yossi had saved up enough money to send Feivel to Harvard.

When vacation came, Yossi grilled his son about the different courses he was taking.

"I take many subjects," said Feivel. "There's French, statistics, and philosophy, to name a few."

"What is this philosophy?" asked Yossi.

"Well, it's difficult to explain," his son answered, "but I'll give you an example. You are now in New York, right?"

"Right!" came the excited reply.

"By using a series of deductions, I can prove to you that you are actually in Pittsburgh. "

Yossi couldn't believe his ears. This was the education he had worked so hard to provide for his son!

Suddenly, Yossi reached over and gave Feivel a sharp slap

across the face.

"What was that for?" cried the astonished boy.

"Now prove your theory," answered Yossi. "Prove to me how I can be in Pittsburgh instead of New York, and then tell me who hit you while I was away!"

ויֵלֶךְ

THIS WEEK IN THE PARSHA

Moshe Transfers Leadership

Moshe tells the people that he is 120 years old, and God has told him he cannot cross the Jordan. But the people must not be afraid. God will help them conquer the Land.

Moshe stands Yehoshua in front of everyone and says, "Be strong and courageous because you will bring this nation to the Land. God leads the way; He will not desert you."

Moshe Gives the Torah

Moshe writes the Torah and gives it to the Levites, and to the elders of B'nai Yisrael.

The Hak'hayl Ceremony

Moshe tells the people that at the end of every seven year Shmita, during the Sukkot festival, the Torah must be read by the leader of the people. It is to be read in the place chosen by God. This is the *Hak'hayl* ceremony, performed "so B'nai Yisrael will learn to fear God, and be careful to fulfill all the Torah."

Moshe Writes A Poem

God tells Moshe that he is about to die and that he should write a poem and teach it to B'nai Yisrael. This poem is to be recited by the Children of Israel for all time.

Moshe writes the poem and teaches it to B'nai Yisrael. He then gives the Torah to the Levites. They are to place it at the side of the Ark as a witness.

Moshe tells the people that he knows they will sin after his death. He wants the elders of the tribes and the officers brought to him so that he can speak to them.

Then he recites the words of the poem to the entire congregation.

THE HAFTARAH CONNECTION

**(Hoshea 14:2-10, Micha 7:18-20,
some people add Yoel 2:15-27)**

This Shabbat is known as *Shabbat Shuva,* "the Shabbat of Repentance," since our Haftarah begins with the phrase *Shuva Yisrael,* "Return people of Israel."

The prophet Hoshea asks B'nai Yisrael to return to God, since they have sinned so much.

This Haftarah is always read on the Shabbat between Rosh Ha'shana and Yom Kippur in order to emphasize the importance of repentance during these days.

1) **Why does the mitzva of reading the Torah every seven years fall out on the holiday of Sukkot?**

2) **Yehoshua is inaugurated by Moshe as the new leader in front of the whole nation. Why did Moshe have to make such a public show?**

3) **After Moshe tells Yehoshua to be strong, for he is now going to lead the nation, Moshe says: "And I will be with you." What is Moshe referring to? After all, didn't God just finish telling him that he was going to die before the nation ever stepped foot in the land?**

WISDOM OF THE SAGES

"And Moshe went and spoke these words..." (31:1)

Why doesn't the Torah tell us where Moshe went?

The Toldot Yitzhak says that the Torah omitted Moshe's destination because wherever he went, be it to work, to do business, or to eat, he always had the same purpose. He was always preaching God's commandments, and conducting himself in a suitable fashion.

"I am 120 years old today." (31:2)

From the word "today," our Sages tell us that Moshe died on his birthday, the seventh of Adar.

"And I will hide my face from you." (31:18)

A story is told of Rabbi Dov of Mezrich. One day he went for a walk in the marketplace and saw a little girl crying. When he asked her why she was crying, she told him that she and her friends had been playing "hide and seek," and since no one was able to find her, they stopped looking. Upon hearing this, the Rabbi started crying. His followers were stunned. The Rabbi explained that this must be how God feels, since we too have stopped looking for him.

No matter how well God hides, he expects us never to stop searching for Him!

GEMMATRIA

Mitzauni ha'raot ha'ayleh, "These evil things have found me." (31:17)

As a result of not listening to God, evil things will happen. The words *ha'raot ha'ayleh*, "these evil things," have the numeric value of 722. This is the same numeric value as the words *Arba galuyot*, "the four exiles" that B'nai Yisrael went through.

God was hinting to B'nai Yisrael that if they didn't listen to Him, they would be repeatedly exiled.

TELL IT WITH A SMILE

This is based on a true story.

A Russian peasant lodged a complaint against his Jewish neighbor, Naftali. It was Sukkot, and the peasant claimed that Naftali had erected a Sukka where it was forbidden for him to do so.

The judge, knowing that the peasant was out to get his neighbor, studied the case very carefully and gave his verdict.

"Naftali," began the judge, "I hereby stipulate that the booth must be taken down — within ten days!"

TABLE TALK
DVAR TORAH

The beginning of our Parsha deals primarily with the change in leadership from Moshe to Yehoshua. The main thing that Moshe tells Yehoshua is that he must not worry, for God is going to walk before him, and will never leave him.

But, in reviewing Jewish history, it would appear that Moshe was mistaken about God never leaving Yehoshua. B'nai Yisrael even lost a war under Yehoshua's leadership. How could this be?

Perhaps this story will help us understand what happened.

One night, a certain man had a dream. In this dream, he was walking along the beach with God. As he was walking, he noticed that the sea was very rough and choppy in some places, while in other places it was calm and serene.

When he looked closer, he could see scenes from his life flashing on the sea. Where the sea was choppy, a sad scene from his life shimmered, where the sea was calm, pleasant scenes from his life appeared.

When the man looked behind him, he saw that parallel with the sea were footprints. He couldn't help but notice that during the low points of his life, there was only one set of footprints in the sand; during the high points in his life, there were two sets of footprints in the sand. This really bothered the man, and he questioned God about it.

"God," the man began, "You promised that once I decided to follow You, You would walk with me, but I notice that during the most troublesome times in my life there is only one set of footprints. I don't understand how, in the times when I needed You most, You abandoned me?"

God replied: "My precious, precious child, I love you very

229

dearly, and I would never ever leave you during your times of trials and suffering. When you see only one set of footprints, it was then that I carried you."

God works in mysterious ways. When we feel downtrodden, and even beaten, we sometimes feel as though God has abandoned us. That is not so. It is with God's help that we manage to overcome our hardships and move on to bigger and better things. And so it was with Yehoshua. Even though he lost the battle, he won the war and went on to conquer the Land.

The Poem of Moshe

Moshe recites a poem, calling the heavens and earth to hear the words he speaks. He begins by praising God, and then asks the people how they have the audacity to rebel.

"Is He not your Father, Who owns you? He created you and molded you," Moshe declares.

"Ask your father and he will tell you; your elders and they will inform you," Moshe says. He recounts what God did for the Jewish people; how He loved them and protected them at every turn.

But, Moshe warns, when God gives B'nai Yisrael what He promised them — a Land flowing with milk and honey — the people will become fat and bloated. Then B'nai Yisrael will desert God and begin worshipping idols. This will anger God. "I will turn My face away from them," God declares. "Then let's see what will be their end."

Moshe then describes the punishments God will mete out.

When the end of B'nai Yisrael seems near, the enemy's conceit will save the people. The enemy will refuse to believe that God has destroyed B'nai Yisrael, and think that they were able to harm the Jewish people through their own gods.

Seeing this, God will have mercy on B'nai Yisrael. The Jewish people will see that the gods who they thought would help them are no-gods. Then God will avenge His people, and they will atone.

The Torah is Life

Moshe concludes the poem and tells the people to make sure to teach the Torah to their children. "For the Torah is not an empty thing for you. It is your life, and with it you will prolong your lives on the Land that you will inherit."

God's Last Reminder To Moshe

Moshe is told to go up Mt. Nevo where he will die. He will not enter the Land of Israel because, when he hit the rock, Moshe rejected the Will of God and did not sanctify Him among the people.

1) Why does Moshe end his speech with such negative imagery and visions?

2) In 32:7 it says to remember the good old days and ask your fathers and elders about them. But didn't the generation of the desert already die out? So who was there to ask?

3) In 32:32 Moshe talks about Sodom and Amora. What connection do these cities have with what Moshe is telling B'nai Yisrael?

 Ha'azeenu ha'shamayim va'adabayra, "Listen heavens and I will speak." (32:1)

Moshe tells the heavens to listen while he speaks. The numerical value of the words *ha'shamayim va'adabayra* is 613, the number of commandments stated in the Torah.

This is to tell us that we too have to listen to the 613 commandments.

232

Our Parsha is basically comprised of the poem that Moshe taught B'nai Yisrael. The poem begins by giving a basic overview concerning B'nai Yisrael's behavior, from the Exodus until the inheritance of the Land. Then, moving into the future, it describes what will happen when the nation becomes too comfortable in the Land. Because of their sins, God will remove Himself from the people and let them fend for themselves. In the end, however, God will come to rescue His nation from the clutches of its enemies.

When referring to the punishment, God says that He will send a *goy nahval,* a "non-believing nation." But in all the other places that God says that He will send a nation to punish B'nai Yisrael, there is no mention of the word "non-believing" to describe that nation. Why is this phrase used here?

The word "non-believing" is used to describe a nation whose driving force is to prove to the world that there is no God. Everything it does focuses around that issue.

The reason this type of nation is used in this case is because of the unique sin committed here. Unlike previous times, when the nation sins because they leave God's path, here, Moshe predicts, "They will not believe in God."

If that is true, then God's punishment makes a great deal of sense. If B'nai Yisrael will sin by denying God's existence, then God will send a nation that also doesn't believe in Him to wipe them out.

Towards the end of the poem, Moshe tells B'nai Yisrael that God will say "Now look, for I am He... I can kill or let live, I can crush and I can cure...."

It is only when these words are engraved in our minds that we can be assured that God will never leave our side.

WISDOM OF THE SAGES

"All His ways are just." (32:4)

The foundation for Judaism is the knowledge that all God's ways are just, even if we don't understand them. We must not behave like children who think the doctor is cruel when he gives them medicine, or that their parents are mean if they punish them.

When the Hafetz Haim once asked someone how he was doing, the man replied that it couldn't hurt to be a little better. The Hafetz Haim said, "How do you know it wouldn't hurt? God is merciful. He knows better than you do what's good for you and what will harm you."

"Your elders and they will tell you." (32:7)

From here we see the importance of the oral law. There are certain things that can only be learned by asking those who lived in the previous generation. Just because it isn't written doesn't mean it's not the truth!

"He and Hoshea the son of Nun." (32:44)

Why is Yehoshua's old name, Hoshea, used here?

To show us that even though Moshe was introducing him to the nation as its new leader, Yehoshua felt that he had not changed, and was still as unworthy as ever to lead the nation.

That is the type of humility that leaders today should aspire to achieve!

TELL IT WITH A SMILE

Moshe tells the heaven and earth to bear witness. In this joke, the earth is called upon once again to bear witness.

During his visit to Rome, Mendel took a tour of the coliseum. The guide got up and announced that the Italians were the first ones to invent the telephone.

"Prove it!" said one of the tourists.

"It's very simple," replied the guide. "While digging in the excavation sites, we found underground wires dating back over 1,000 years!"

"That's nothing," Mendel said. "We Jews invented the cordless phone."

Again the same tourist shouted, "Prove it!"

"Simple," began Mendel. "When digging in our excavation sites, which date back almost 2,000 years, we didn't find any wires!"

THE HAFTARAH CONNECTION

(Shmuel II, 22:1-51)

Our Parsha consists of Moshe's last poem of praise to God, before "going to meet his Maker."

In the Haftarah, we read of a song sung by King David in praise of God, after God delivered him from his enemies.

וזאת הברכה

Moshe Blesses the Tribes

Before his death, Moshe blesses B'nai Yisrael. He recalls how God had appeared at Mt. Sinai and gave them the Torah, and how they had accepted it saying, "The Torah that Moshe commanded us is the inheritance of the Congregation of Yaacov."

Then he blesses the tribes, describing their traits. Moshe concludes by telling the people how fortunate they are that God is their shield and their deliverer in times of trouble.

The Death of Moshe

Moshe goes up Mt. Nevo, and God shows him the Land. God tells Moshe, "This is the Land that I swore to give to the descendants of Avraham, Yitzhak, and Yaacov. I have let you see it, but you cannot cross over to the Land."

Moshe, the servant of God, dies on the mountain, in the Land of Moav. He is buried in the valley. To this day, no one knows his precise burial place.

At his death he was 120 years old; his eyesight had not dimmed, and his energy had not decreased.

B'nai Yisrael mourn Moshe for 30 days.

Yehoshua becomes the leader, and the people obey him.

There would never again appear a prophet like Moshe, who

knew God face to face, and performed such wonders in front of B'nai Yisrael.

THE HAFTARAH CONNECTION

(Yehoshua 1:1-18)

This week, we read of Moshe's swan song and his subsequent death.

Our Haftarah is taken from the first chapter of Yehoshua, the first book of the prophets. Even though Moshe died, B'nai Yisrael haven't stopped functioning. Yehoshua, their new leader, will pick up where Moshe left off and lead B'nai Yisrael into the promised Land.

FOOD FOR THOUGHT

1) Why wasn't Moshe's burial place made public knowledge?

2) Compare Moshe's blessing of the tribes to Yaacov's blessing of his sons in B'raishit 49.

3) What was so special about Binyamin that he was described by Moshe as the "friend of God?" (33:12)

GEMMATRIA

Torah tziva lanu Moshe, "Moshe commanded us the Torah..." (33:4)

The Hebrew word, *Torah*, has the numeric value of 611. This comes to tell us that B'nai Yisrael heard 611 of God's commandments through Moshe. The other two, which were the first two of the Ten Commandments, B'nai Yisrael heard directly from God.

In the blessing given to Levi, the tribe whose job it is to teach the Torah, Moshe says to pay close attention to three things (33:9):

First, the influence of parents. Parents have a very strong influence on their children. Our personalities are formed under the careful supervision of our parents, and it is thanks to them that we are aware of the positive things we must do.

Second, the influence of siblings and friends. This refers to society. We can be influenced by society so that we forget everything our parents have taught us and stray from the correct path. On the other hand, society can help us take our basic skills, refine them, and elevate them to a higher level.

Third, the importance of children. This is the final test of how well we have internalized everything we were taught as children. If we can now pass it on to the next generation, then we can say that we have successfully overcome the hurdles that life has put in our path.

With this week's Parsha, we finish reading the Torah, and celebrate the holiday of *Simhat Torah*. We can now look back and see what we have learned in from the past year. The Torah we have read throughout the year symbolizes our parents. From the Torah we have absorbed in the important messages we need to grow as Jews in this world.

When we dance around with the Torah, we do it together with our friends. These are the people who influence us in our everyday life. We must strive to meld their positive traits with our own, so that we can continue our pattern of Torah growth.

Last, but not least, we begin reading the Torah again from B'raishit, symbolizing the passing of the Torah to the next generation — the ultimate goal in our life. This is a new opportunity to learn and to grow, an opportunity we must all take to heart.

That is why Simhat Torah is so special. It combines the past, present, and future, to show us the proper way of serving God.

WISDOM OF THE SAGES

"And this is the blessing which Moshe blessed..." (33:1)

The previous Parsha ended with God telling Moshe that he would not be the one leading B'nai Yisrael into the Land of Israel. Yet, even though Moshe blamed B'nai Yisrael for his punishment (3:26), he blessed them anyway.

This illustrates the devotion and love Moshe had for the people.

"Moshe commanded us the Torah, a legacy of the Congregation of Yaacov." (33:4)

How can we keep *all* the commandments when some of them apply only to specific segments of the community, such as the Kohanim and Levites?

That is why the second half of the verse refers to B'nai Yisrael as "the Congregation of Yaacov." It declares that there is a unity to be found within the Jewish people. If the Kohen performs his job, it is as if the whole community did it.

"Let Reuven live and not die." (33:6)

Why was Reuven singled out to "live and not die?"

In return for the land on the "other side of the Jordan river," the tribes of Reuven, Gad, and half of Menashe promised to lead the battle in Israel. Reuven, who was always in the front ranks, needed the special blessing of life in order to survive.

Mrs. Hotselpfeffer suddenly became very ill right after celebrating her 104th birthday. One of her great-great-grandchildren quickly took her to the doctor.

"You'll make me better, won't you?" asked Mrs. Hotselpfeffer.

The kind doctor took her hand and tried to sooth her. "When one is past the century mark, all kinds of little ailments, aches, and pains, happen. You must understand, that I am a doctor, not a magician. I can't make you any younger."

"Younger?" she cried out hysterically. "Who wants to be younger? I just want you to help me get older – lots older!"

ABOUT THE
HOLIDAYS

PESAH

SHAVUOT

ROSH HA'SHANA

YOM KIPPUR

SUKKOT

SIMHAT TORAH

Pesah

The Pesah Festival, called Passover in English, is an eight-day holiday (seven days in Israel) beginning on the 15th day of the Hebrew month *Nissan.* This is the first of the *Shalosh Regalim,* "Three Festivals," mentioned in the Torah.

This holiday serves as a commemoration of the fact that God took B'nai Yisrael out of Egypt.

God commanded B'nai Yisrael to slaughter a sheep on the 14th day of Nissan and to smear its blood on the doorpost of their houses. The houses with blood on their doorposts were saved when God killed the firstborn of Egypt.

Following this plague, B'nai Yisrael rushed out of Egypt. The bread they baked for their exodus did not have enough time to rise, which is why unleavened bread, called *matza*, is eaten on Pesah.

Most of the things done on Pesah are intended to remind us of the Exodus from Egypt.

On the first two days and the last two days of Pesah, no work is allowed to be done. The four days in between are called *hol ha'moed* – "the weekday holiday." They don't have most of the restrictions of a holiday, but are not a total weekday either.

 The Torah Reading

On each of the eight days of Pesah, we read a different portion from the Torah.

FIRST DAY: Reading – Shemot 12:21-51
Maftir – B'midbar 28:16-25
Haftarah – Yehoshua 5:2-6:1, 7:1

This portion relates to the events that precede the Exodus, and continues with the plague of the firstborn and the Exodus itself. It concludes with the different laws involved in eating the Passover lamb.

The Maftir portion for this day, as well as for the other days, describes the sacrifices of the day brought in the Sanctuary.

In the Haftarah, we read of the Pesah that B'nai Yisrael celebrated before beginning to fight for the Land of Israel.

SECOND DAY: Va'yikra – 22:26-23:44
Maftir – B'midbar 28:16-25
Haftarah – Melahim II 23:1-9,21-25

The Torah reading enumerates a number of laws pertaining to sacrifices. It also warns the people not to profane God's name "because He took us out of Egypt." This is followed by a brief explanation of Shabbat, Pesah, Shavuot, Yom Kippur, and Sukkot.

In the Haftarah, we read how King Yosheyahu commands B'nai Yisrael to keep Pesah. This is their first Pesah since the reign of the Judges.

THIRD DAY: Shemot 13:1-16
Maftir – B'midbar 28:19-25

We read about the laws pertaining to firstborn humans and animals. There is a commandment to remember the Exodus, especially when entering the Land of Israel. One way of doing this is to educate the children; another way is to maintain a bond with God by wearing Tefillin.

FOURTH DAY: Shemot 22:24-23:19
Maftir – B'midbar 28:19-25

We begin by reading different laws ranging from the law of giving charity to laws pertaining to the actions of judges. We conclude with reading about Pesah, Shavuot, and Sukkot, and the commandment to go to Jerusalem and bring sacrifices during these holidays.

FIFTH DAY: Shemot 34:1-26
Maftir – B'midbar 28:19-25
We read about the new covenant that God made with B'nai Yisrael after they sinned by worshipping the Golden Calf.

SIXTH DAY: B'midbar 9:1-14
Maftir – B'midbar 28:19-25
We read of the special laws pertaining to *Pesah Sheni*, "the Second Pesah." All those who couldn't bring the Pesah lamb during the proper time, either because they were impure or because they were too far away, could bring it one month later, on the 15th of *Iyar*.

SHABBAT HOL HA'MOED: Shir Ha'shirim
Shemot 33:12-34:26
Haftarah – Yehezkel 36:37-37:14
Shir Ha'shirim – "The Song of Songs," is a love song composed by *Shlomo Ha'meleh*, "King Solomon." It describes, allegorically, the love of B'nai Yisrael for God. This is a very appropriate song to sing to God on the day that He freed us from our slavery.

The Torah portion begins with Moshe's request to see God's grandeur. God tells Moshe that no one can see Him and live. He ends up putting Moshe into the cleft of a rock and showing him a vision.

The reading then goes on to deal with the new covenant God made with B'nai Yisrael after the sin of the Golden Calf.

God gives B'nai Yisrael a list of commandments that they must do when they enter the Land of Israel. In return, God promises to help them defeat their enemies and widen their borders. This will enable them to travel safely to Jerusalem during the Three Festivals.

The Haftarah deals with Yehezkel's prophecy about the "dry bones." In this prophecy, bones that are left in the field suddenly appear to "grow" new flesh on them and are filled with life. God tells Yehezkel that He will also open our graves and bring us up to the Land of Israel. This is read on Pesah because the Exodus portrays the revival of the Jewish people, and how God brought them into the Land of Israel.

SEVENTH DAY: Shemot 13:17-15:26
Haftarah – Shmuel II 22:1-51
We read of the Exodus from Egypt and the miracle of the splitting of the Red Sea. The Torah reading continues with the song of praise that B'nai Yisrael sang to God after they crossed the sea safely. It concludes with the miracle that God did, showing Moshe how to sweeten the bitter waters when B'nai Yisrael complained of thirst.

EIGHTH DAY: When it falls out on a Shabbat, read
Shemot 14:22-16:17. When it falls out on a weekday,
read Shemot 15:19- 16:17
Haftarah – Yeshayahu 10:32-12:6
The Torah reading begins by telling us the importance of giving charity and helping one another. It concludes by summarizing the Three Festivals.

In the Haftarah, we read about the famous prophecy of "The wolf shall dwell with the lamb, and the leopard shall lie down with the kid." It describes the peaceful co-existence that is to occur when we are once again redeemed from exile.

TABLE TALK
DVAR TORAH

The word Pesah can have two meanings: *Pesah*, "passed over," and *Pe sah*, which means "the mouth talks."

These two interpretations are the two focal points of this festival.

The first, refers to the historical aspect of what took place in Egypt, how God passed over all the Jewish houses when he destroyed the Egyptian firstborn. This is proof to us that God constantly keeps an eye out for His nation.

The second aspect "the mouth talks," relates to the need for us to talk about the miracles that occurred. It is important to note that the present tense is used here. This indicates that as far as Pesah is concerned, a Jew cannot be silent. He must always be ready to tell the story of the Exodus.

When Yaacov dressed up in his brother's, Esav's, clothes in order to receive the blessings, his father Yitzhak first felt Yaacov's hands. He then proclaimed: "The voice is the voice of Yaacov, and the hands are the hands of Esav."

The voice tells tales of the past, stresses the challenges of the present, and raises hopes for the future.

This voice is brought into play on Pesah. On this day, we sit at the table, read the *Haggadah* and talk about the miracle of Pesah — how God passed over our houses in Egypt and saved us from death. The present is also stressed by our eating matza and bitter herbs, and by our drinking wine. At the end of the meal we express our hope for the future by singing and proclaiming:

"Next Year in the Rebuilt Jerusalem."

FOR YOUR INFORMATION

1) The night before Pesah we do *bedikat hametz*, "checking for leavened bread". This is done by going from room to room with a candle, checking for anything that might have been missed during the "Pesah cleaning." In some houses it is customary to give the children ten pieces of bread to hide around the house.

2) The next morning we do *biur hametz*, "destroying leavened bread." We must get rid of any and all hametz in our possession. This can be done by either selling it, burning it, or throwing it into the wind.

3) During Pesah, it is forbidden to eat *hametz*, "leavened bread." This includes anything made of flour and water which is left to rise for more than 18 minutes.

4) We eat *matza*, "unleavened bread," also known as poor man's bread. We do this in order to commemorate the matza we had to eat when we left Egypt. At that time we couldn't wait for the dough to rise.

5) On the first night of Pesah we are commanded to eat matza, and to drink four cups of wine. The four cups correspond to the four different phrases used for redemption. We are to eat the matza, and drink the wine while leaning to the left, as a symbol of freedom. In ancient times it was customary for all free men to lean while eating.

6) The Haggadah is read on the first and second night during the meal called *Seder*, which means "order." The meal was given this name since everything is done in a certain order in the Haggadah. The Haggadah itself is divided into 15 parts. The purpose of the Haggadah is to educate others about what happened in Egypt, and to reenact the Exodus. It stresses the

fact that if God had not taken us out of Egypt, we would still be enslaved there to this very day.

7) On the Seder night, we eat bitter herbs reminding us of the bitterness we had to endure while enslaved in Egypt.

8) During the Seder, we pour a fifth cup of wine known as "Eliyahu's cup." This cup is left on the table while the door is opened to let the prophet Eliyahu in. It is this prophet who will one day bring the redemption.

9) The complete Hallel prayer is recited on the first two days. In some congregations it is even recited at night. During the rest of the days, we only say what is known as the "half Hallel" prayer.

10) The prayer for dew is recited during the repetition of the Musaf prayer on the first day.

WISDOM OF THE SAGES

If you've ever seen matza being made, you'll notice that it is a frantic race against the clock; kneading, rolling and baking, all must be completed within the span of 18 minutes. If the dough is left for longer than 18 minutes, it rises, and becomes hametz.

The Vilna Gaon says that a man's personality is very much like this matza process. Someone who is constantly doing things, involved in constructive activities, doesn't have time to "rise," to become selfish or proud. However, if he just lazes about and wastes precious time, then, like the bread that begins to rise, he too will become "full of himself."

Shavuot

The holiday of Shavuot is a two-day holiday which falls out on the sixth day of the month of *Sivan*. This day commemorates the day that B'nai Yisrael received the Torah on Mt. Sinai.

In addition, it is also the conclusion of the *Omer* period, a counting of 50 days, beginning the second night of Pesah and ending on Shavuot. We count seven full weeks during the Omer period. That is why the holiday is called, Shavuot, which means "weeks."

WISDOM OF THE SAGES

Shavuot is the only holiday from the Torah whose date isn't specified. We celebrate it on the sixth of Sivan, but it says in the Torah that it occurs on the 50th day of the counting of the Omer. Why is the date not mentioned?

We learn from this that the date of the giving of the Torah, in and of itself, has very little meaning. God doesn't want us to feel as if the Torah was given once, and that's it! He wants us to feel as if we receive the Torah anew every single day. Every time we are taught something new, be it from our teachers or from our parents, we should feel as if we are receiving the Torah.

 # The Torah Reading

First day: The first thing that is read on Shavuot is usually the Megila of Ruth. One of the many different reasons given for reading the Megila today is to show us that sometimes the Torah can best be appreciated when a person is in great despair. It was during her worst ordeals that Ruth shone in her modest and humble ways. She started the greatest lineage of leadership the nation has ever seen.

In the Torah, we read from Shemot 19:1. This is very appropriate since it talks about Moshe going up to Mt. Sinai to get the Torah, and today is actually the anniversary of that day.

The Maftir is read from B'midbar 28:26. This deals with the sacrifices that were brought on Shavuot.

The Haftarah is read from Yehezkel 1:1

This is probably the toughest passage to understand in the Prophets. It is a prophecy revealed during the exile, which came about as a result of the people not fulfilling the Torah. We can rectify this by adhering to the Torah given on this very day.

Second day: When it falls out on Shabbat, we read from Devarim 14:22-16:17. When it falls out on a weekday, we from Devarim 15:19- 16:17.

We read about the importance of helping out a fellow man, and about the Shalosh Regalim, which includes Shavuot.

The Maftir is the same as on the first day.

The Haftarah — Habakuk 2:20-3:19

Here the prophet Habakuk reveals God's greatness. Just like the revelation on Mt. Sinai was the point of entry for God among the Jewish people, so too here, God's entry into all of mankind is envisioned in this reading.

FOR YOUR INFORMATION

1) Before reading the Megila, two blessings are recited.

A. *Baruh atta...al mikra megila.*

B. *Baruh atta...she'he'heyanu v'keyemanu v'hegeyanu la'zman ha'ze.*

2) During the prayers, we recite the complete Hallel prayer.

3) It is customary to decorate the synagogue and home with flowers and green plants. This is done to celebrate the giving of the Torah, which took place on a green mountain.

4) It is customary to eat milk products on Shavuot. One reason is that until B'nai Yisrael received the Torah, they ate non-kosher animals, and animals that weren't slaughtered properly. After the Torah was given, they could no longer use those same vessels to cook in. Therefore, they had no choice but to eat milk products. We commemorate this experience by eating milk products on this day.

5) Many people stay up all night learning Torah. They do this because Shavuot is a wedding or unification between God and B'nai Yisrael. It is only right that we stay up all night preparing for this experience.

6) Before the Torah reading, in certain congregations it is customary to say the *Akdamot.* This is a poem of praise to God, the Torah, and B'nai Yisrael. It is written in Aramaic, and consists of 90 rhyming sentences. Each sentence ends with the two Hebrew letters *Taf,* the last letter of the Hebrew alphabet, and *Alef,* the first letter in the alphabet. This symbolizes the fact that after finishing the Torah, we must begin studying it once again.

7) This holiday has four different names:

A. *Hag Ha'katzir,* "the holiday of harvest," for this is the agricultural time of harvest.

B. *Shavuot,* "weeks," because today we finish counting the weeks from Pesah to Shavuot.

C. *Atzeret,* "stop," which is symbolic of the fact that Shavuot is considered the last day of Pesah. Only today, with the giving of the Torah, does Pesah — the Exodus — actually come to a stop.

D. *Yom Ha'bikurim,* "the day of the first fruits," because starting from this day, B'nai Yisrael had to bring their first fruit to God.

TABLE TALK
DVAR TORAH

Today's Torah reading begins with the verse: "The third month after B'nai Yisrael left Egypt..." (Shemot 19:1)

Why is this prelude to the giving of the Torah necessary?

It is obvious from here that there is a very distinct connection between leaving Egypt and receiving the Torah.

We know that Pesah, the redemption from Egypt, and Shavuot, the receiving of the Torah, are connected, because we begin counting the days of the Omer on the second day of Pesah, and conclude on Shavuot.

It would seem that one event is actually a continuation of the other. B'nai Yisrael needed to be physically removed from slavery, but just leaving Egypt was not enough to make them a unified nation. They also needed a spiritual redemption as well. This redemption came in the form of the Torah, which showed them how to live as a free people under the yoke of God.

This whole process can be compared to that of an egg. All eggs undergo two births. The first is when the egg leaves the chicken's body, and the second is when it hatches. B'nai Yisrael were born into the world when they left Egypt, but they still had the shell of slavery around them. They became fully alive when they received the Torah.

When we count the days of the Omer, we count from 1 to 49, symbolizing how one event leads to the next. In the process, we slowly gain spirituality and holiness, until we reach maturity on the 50th day.

Rosh Ha'shana

Rosh Ha'shana is a two-day holiday beginning on the first day of the Hebrew month *Tishray*. The phrase, Rosh Ha'shana, literally means "New Year." On this holiday no work is allowed to be done.

Of special importance is the fact that God begins judging us on Rosh Ha'shana.

On Rosh Ha'shana, 100 blasts of the *shofar,* "ram's horn" are sounded. One of the reasons for blowing the shofar is so these loud blasts will wake us from our spiritual slumber and remind us that we must do *teshuva,* "repentance," at once.

WISDOM OF THE SAGES Rosh Ha'shana teaches us how to approach something new. While the rest of the world celebrates the "New Year" with firecrackers and non-stop partying, we see it as a time of reflection. It is a time set aside for us to see what we've done during the past year and how we can improve during the coming year.

So too, any new beginning, like a birthday or the start of the new school year, should be looked upon as a time to stop and reflect on how we can make this a better year!

TABLE TALK DVAR TORAH

There are many reasons given as to why we blow the shofar on Rosh Ha'shana. One of the reasons can best be expressed by a parable which Rav Yehuda Amital of Yeshivat Har Etzion is fond of telling.

Many years ago in Europe, there lived a Rabbi whose fame had spread far and wide.

Leibish, an old friend of the Rabbi, decides that he wants to spend a Shabbat with his dear, old friend. He writes a letter asking for permission to come and is ecstatic when the Rabbi sends back a message that he is waiting with open arms.

After a long journey, Leibish arrives at the Rabbi's house where the two friends joyously greet each other.

Leibish accompanies the Rabbi to the local mikva, where they both immerse themselves, purifying themselves in preparation for Shabbat. After dressing themselves in their beautiful Shabbat clothes, they go to the study where they begin learning. An hour passes, and then, all of a sudden, somebody comes barging through the door. Leibish is astonished to see a filthy peasant dressed in torn rags, standing at the door. The peasant starts screaming, "Rabbi, Rabbi."

"What do you want?" asks the Rabbi, calmly.

"Well," begins the peasant, "My cow has become very ill, and she won't give any milk. I'm afraid that she may die."

"Don't worry," the Rabbi tells him, "Just keep the cow warm, make sure she drinks plenty of chicken soup, and gets some rest."

The peasant embraces the Rabbi, showering him with words of praise, and then promptly turns and leaves.

Leibish, bewildered by what happened, asks the Rabbi to explain.

"Every year," the Rabbi says, "this peasant comes barging in to ask me questions about his livestock. He wants to be able to communicate with me, but he's illiterate and feels he has no common ground to be able to talk to me. Therefore he asks me about things that he knows — livestock. He doesn't expect me to solve his problems, it's just an excuse to come talk to me."

This is also the case with the shofar on Rosh Ha'shana. Not

everyone knows how to read from a *siddur.* The prayers that we recite don't strike the spiritual chords of some people. That is why, on this special day, we are given another way of communicating with God, the shofar.

When we hear the shofar, not words, but emotions become the tools with which we contact God. We open our hearts and cry out, sending our deepest feelings soaring on the sounds of the shofar. For many this is the way they can best communicate with God. It is their way of making conversation with their Maker.

May the prayers of our lips and our souls help us merit a year of blessing in the "Book of Life."

 # FOR YOUR INFORMATION

1) The shofar is sounded on both the first and second day. The best type of shofar is that which comes from a ram, because of the ram that was slaughtered by Avraham at the *Akaida,* instead of Yitzhak.

2) There are two blessings recited prior to blowing the shofar:

A. *Baruh atta...Li'shmoa kol shofar.*

B. *Baruh atta...She'he'heyanu v'keyemanu v'hegeyanu la'zman ha'ze.*

From the first blessing until the last sound of the shofar, it is forbidden to talk.

3) There are many customs on Rosh Ha'shana which symbolize our hopes for the upcoming year:

A. We stay awake all day so as not to have a "sleepy year."

B. We eat certain symbolic fruits throughout the meal. For example, the head of a fish is eaten to symbolize that we will always be like a "head," staying on top of things and not falling behind. A pomegranate is also eaten. This symbolizes that we want our merits to be as numerous as the pomegranate seeds.

4) We read the prayers of *tashlih,* which means "to throw away." The congregation gathers at an ocean, river, or body of natural water, and recites certain passages from the Psalms. In addition, they shake out their pockets. Some people even throw bread into the water to symbolize the fact that they are ridding themselves of all sins. This is usually done on the first day, after the Minha prayer.

5) It is customary on the second night to have something new: a fruit that hasn't been eaten that year or new clothes. This is done in order to enable us to recite the *She'he'heyanu* blessing on the second night as well as the first night of Rosh Ha'shana.

🕮 The Torah Reading

FIRST DAY: We read from B'raishit 21:1, which deals with Sarah giving birth to Yitzhak.

Our Rabbis tell us that it was on Rosh Ha'shana that God "remembered" Sarah, and allowed her to conceive her first child at the age of ninety.

The rest of the Torah reading deals with Avraham telling Hagar and Yishmael to leave the house, since they were a bad influence on his son Yitzhak.

It is especially important that on Rosh Hashana we remember to stay away from people who may be a bad influence on us.

The Maftir is read from B'midbar 29:1, which deals with the sacrifices brought on this day.

The Haftarah is taken from Shmuel I 1:1

We read the story of Hana, a woman who has trouble conceiving. Like Sarah, she is a great woman and God listens to her prayers and blesses her with a child. The child becomes Shmuel, the prophet.

SECOND DAY: We read from B'raishit 22:1, which deals with the *Akaida*, "the binding" of Yitzhak.

As we know, Avraham almost sacrificed his son Yitzhak, but at the last second he was commanded not to. Instead, he took a ram and sacrificed it.

The ram's horn is sounded because we want God to remember the test that Avraham passed and use it in our merit.

The Maftir is the same as on the first day.

The Haftarah is taken from Yermeyahu 31:1

We read of a prophecy filled with hope and happiness. It reveals a future time when B'nai Yisrael will be reunited as a result of their merits.

We want to remind God of these merits during these crucial days.

Yom Kippur

Yom Kippur is a 25 hour fast day that falls out on the 10th day of the Hebrew month of *Tishray*. Yom Kippur is also known as

Yom Hadin, "the Day of Judgment," for this is the day when our fate for the coming year is signed and sealed.

FOR YOUR INFORMATION

1) On the day before Yom Kippur there is a custom to carry out the ritual of *kaparot,* which means "atonement." This is commonly done by putting money in a bag and swinging it over your head, while reciting a prayer that your sins should be transferred to the money. The money is then given to charity.

2) During the *Minha,* afternoon prayer before Yom Kippur, the *viduy,* called the "confession" prayer is recited. In it, we list our sins and ask for forgiveness. After Minha, a special meal called the *seuda mafseket* is eaten.

3) Some people make sure to go to the local mikva just before Yom Kippur begins, in order to purify themselves.

4) There are five things that are prohibited on Yom Kippur:

A. Food and drink
B. Washing up
C. Wearing leather shoes
D. Rubbing your body with oil
E. Intimate relations

 # The Torah Reading

The Torah is read twice on this day. Once, during *Shaharit,* the morning prayers: Va'yikra 16:1-34

Maftir – B'midbar 29:7-11

Haftarah– Yeshayahu 57:14-58:14

The Torah reading explains the procedure that the Kohen Gadol has to follow for the Yom Kippur service in the Sanctuary.

In the Maftir we read about the special sacrifice of the day that was brought.

Our Haftarah begins with the words "Rise up, rise up.."

This is a fitting call on the day when we are trying to get closer to God. The prophet Yeshayahu points out that God promised to help us as soon as we repent.

During Minha prayers we read: Va'yikra 18:1-30

Haftarah – The Book of Yona.

The Torah reading during Minha is taken from the same Parsha as that of Shaharit. We read that we shouldn't be like the other nations that surround us, instead, we must detest all abominations. That is the only way that we can be sure to remain in the same state of holiness that we have achieved today.

For the Haftarah, we read the Book of Yona. There are two important lessons we learn from this book. The first is that there is no running away from God. The second important lesson is the power of *teshuva,* "repentance." The people of Ninve were about to be annihilated, but once they did teshuva, they were forgiven for their sins.

WISDOM OF THE SAGES There are many different ways of getting our messages to God. Each message goes through a certain "gate". Of all the gates, there is one that is extremely important on this day, the "Gate of Tears." It is unusual because it is always open. Even when *Neila,* the "closing service" of Yom Kippur arrives at the end of the day, the Gate of Tears stays steadfastly opened. Every tear we shed is collected and counted, and used in our defense in the "High Court of Justice."

TABLE TALK DVAR TORAH

The main focal point of Yom Kippur is our ability to do teshuva. It is truly an amazing thing. One minute we can be "out of sorts" with God because of the many sins in our past, and the next minute, if we repent, we can be close to God.

This is a kindness that should not be taken for granted. There is really no logical explanation for it. In truth, if someone does something wrong, he should be punished for his evil doings. Repentance should not be able to erase those sins as if they had never occurred.

The Tractate Brahot 34b says that "Where those who do teshuva stand, perfect righteous people can't stand." How can such a thing be?

There are two ways of understanding this:

If a king has two servants, one of whom had sinned and repented, and the other one who had never done anything wrong, which one is the king more likely to favor?

The king will favor the one who did wrong and repented. The reason for this is that the king now knows that this particular servant is reliable. He was tempted, failed, and in the end, returned. The king can now safely predict that this servant won't let him down again. However, regarding the other servant, the king has no idea what will happen if he sins. Will the servant repent or not?

When we repent after sinning, it increases our value in God's eye, because He knows that we make sure not to do the same sins again.

The other way of understanding this question of sinner versus non-sinner, is to visualize a rope that connects man to God. As man sins, more and more strands in the rope begin to unwind, causing him to become more and more separated from God. However, when he finally does teshuva, the connection isn't only re-established, it is even closer. The reason for this is that God ties knots in the rope wherever the strings began to unwind, resulting in a shorter rope, and thus, a closer connection to God.

May we all merit to become *ba'alay teshuva,* "people who repent", and in doing so, solidify our connection with God.

Gmar hatima tova, we should all be sealed in the book of life!

Sukkot

Sukkot is an eight-day holiday (seven days in Israel) which begins on the 15th of the Hebrew month *Tishray.*

The holiday is celebrated by moving from our houses to a *sukka,* "a hut." This move commemorates the fact that B'nai Yisrael lived in huts when they left Egypt.

On Sukkot we take the *arba minim,* "the four species." These include a lulav, etrog, three hadasim, and two aravot.

The seventh day of Sukkot is known as *Hoshana Rabba.* It is the last day on which we use our arba minim.

The last day of Sukkot is called *Shemini Atzeret,* "the eighth day of remaining." God added this day to the seven days of Sukkot. We remain with God for an extra day.

The first two days, as well as the last two days, are days in which no work is allowed to be done. The four days in between are *hol ha'moed* (see Pesah for further elaboration).

WISDOM OF THE SAGES

The Talmud says that the reason for an extra day of Sukkot, is that after seven days we form such a special relationship with God, that He doesn't want us to leave Him. So He created an extra holy day.

The obvious question is: if it's hard to depart after seven days, won't it be much more difficult to do so after eight?

The Shem Mi'shmuel says that numbers play an important role in this case. Seven is a number that signifies nature, and all things natural, as we see from the seven days of the week. One of the laws of nature is that we forget things, even events that are important to us. The number eight, on the other hand, is one above nature. Forgetting is not within this number's reference.

God didn't want our relationship to end after seven days, because then it would be easier for us to forget Him. Now that the holiday is celebrated for eight days, the memory of it should be enough to strengthen us for the year to come.

TABLE TALK
DVAR TORAH

Sukkot is considered the last of the three major holidays; Pesah, Shavuot, and Sukkot. There are many similarities between these three holidays. For example, during the time of the Temple, there was a mass pilgrimage to Jerusalem during these festivals. Also, the *Hallel* prayer is read in synagogue. Finally, they all share the mitzva of happiness.

Our Sages point out that Sukkot has a unique characteristic. It is part of the teshuva process which began with Rosh Ha'shana. On Yom Kippur, we are forgiven for our sins, and from then until Sukkot we busy ourselves with accumulating as many mitzvot as we possibly can. Then, during Sukkot, all of B'nai Yisrael stand before God with their lulav, as if they have just returned victorious from war, and show their complete acceptance of God and His Torah.

This brings us to the question of whether Sukkot should be considered part of the Shalosh Regalim, or part of the holidays in the month of Tishray?

Actually, Sukkot has both these aspects.

As one of the Shalosh Regalim, Sukkot has an agricultural element. While Pesah is the time of planting, and Shavuot is the time of the first fruit, Sukkot celebrates the long-awaited harvest. It is the end of the year, when we reap the fruits of our labor.

And Sukkot is also the end of the teshuva process, which started with shedding tears of sadness during Rosh Ha'shana and Yom Kippur, and culminates with tears of joy to God on Sukkot.

So we see that the joy of Sukkot is two-fold: We thank God for letting us reap our fruits, and for forgiving our sins.

May the coming year be a continuation of this joyous time!

 # The Torah Reading

THE FIRST DAY: Torah reading- Va'yikra 22:26-23:44.

Maftir — B'midbar 28:12-16.

Haftarah — Zeharia 14 1-21

The Torah reading discusses the Shalosh Regalim: Pesah, Shavuot, and Sukkot.

The Maftir reviews the sacrifices brought on this day.

The Haftarah mentions three times that the goal of mankind is for the nations to come up yearly to Jerusalem and bow down before God, celebrating the festival of Sukkot.

THE SECOND DAY: The Torah and Maftir are the same as the first day.

Haftarah – Melahim I 8:2-21

The Haftarah deals with the consecration of the first Temple, during the festival of Sukkot.

HOL HA'MOED: During the four days of hol ha'moed, we read from B'midbar 29:12-34 about the sacrifices that were brought.

SHABBAT HOL HA'MOED: Torah reading - Shemot 33:12-34:26

Maftir – This depends on what day of hol ha'moed Shabbat falls.

Haftarah – Yehezkel 38:18-39:16

The Torah portion begins with Moshe's request to see God's grandeur. God tells Moshe that no one can see Him and live. God does put Moshe into the cleft of a rock and shows him a vision.

The reading then deals with the new covenant between God and B'nai Yisrael after they sinned by worshipping the Golden Calf. God gives B'nai Yisrael a list of commandments that He wants them to keep when they enter the Land of Israel. In return, God promises to help B'nai Yisrael defeat their enemies and widen their borders. Then the people will be able to travel securely to Jerusalem during the Three Festivals.

The Haftarah depicts the final, decisive battle, at the end of days, which will bestow permanent peace and happiness for everyone. The sign of victory will be the arrival of the "united nations" up to Jerusalem to declare their loyalty to God. This takes place during Sukkot.

SHEMINI ATZERET: Torah reading – Devarim 14:22-16:17
Maftir — B'midbar 29:35-30:1
Haftarah – Melahim I 8:54-9:1

The Torah reading begins by telling us the importance of giving charity and helping someone in distress. It then goes on to talk about the Shalosh Regalim, which include Sukkot.

In the Maftir, we read about the offerings brought on this day.

This Haftarah describes the end of the consecration of the First Temple, which we started reading about on the first day. On Shemini Atzeret the nation departed from King Shlomo, after having spent eight glorious days together.

FOR YOUR INFORMATION

1) The sukka that is built for this holiday, must be a temporary structure.

2) It is customary to decorate the sukka with ornaments.

3) On each day of Sukkot we invite the *ushpizin*, Aramaic for "guests," into our sukka. Every night we formally call on one of them to lead the others. These are important people from our past: Avraham, Yitzhak, Yaacov, Moshe, Aaron, Yosef, and David.

4) The arba minim are set up as follows: The aravot and hadassim are tied to the lulav. The aravot are on the left and the hadassim on the right. The lulav is then held in the right hand, and the etrog in the left.

5) When we make the blessing on the arba minim, we first take the etrog and hold it upside down, take the remaining arba minim and make the blessing, and then turn the etrog right-side-up. We shake the arba minim in six directions (north, east, south, west, up, down).

6) During Sukkot, we celebrate the *simhat bait ha'showeva,* "the water libation ceremony" that used to take place in the Temple. The Talmud tells us that "whoever never witnessed the simhat bait ha'showeva, never saw true rejoicing in his life."

7) After Hallel, we take out a Torah from the Ark, and put it on the *bima*. We then walk around it with our arba minim and recite the *Hoshana*, a request for God to "save us." On the last day of hol ha'moed, also known as *Hoshana Rabba,* we circle the bima seven times.

8) The prayer for rain is recited during the repetition of the Musaf prayer on Shemini Atzeret.

Simhat Torah

This holiday falls out on the 23rd of the hebrew month of *Tishray*. In Israel, this holiday is celebrated on the 22nd, together with *Shemini Atzeret*.

On this holiday we celebrate the completion of the yearly cycle of the Torah reading. We celebrate by reading the last Parsha, and then begin again with the first Parsha of B'raishit.

WISDOM OF THE SAGES

What do the words Simhat Torah mean? They mean, "The rejoicing of the Torah." This teaches us an important lesson about how to learn Torah: We should make sure that we rejoice in the learning of Torah.

TABLE TALK DVAR TORAH

Right after we finish the Book of Devarim, we begin again by reading from B'raishit. This is the only occasion when we read an entire Parsha and, immediately afterward, begin another Parsha – but do not read it to the end.

If we are not going to finish B'raishit, why start it? What's the rush?

In effect, we are declaring that we will never stop learning. We will never "finish." There is always more to be learned by reviewing one more time. Every year, when we read the Parsha, we have new insights that we overlooked the previous year.

Our Sages say that "One who doesn't review, is like someone who ploughs and plants but doesn't harvest." All the work and effort we put into learning it the first time is wasted if we don't review it.

The Tractate Hagiga 9b states that "You can't compare someone who reviews something 100 times to someone who reviews something 101 times." Is there really a difference between the 100th and 101st time?

Yes, there is! The Talmud is trying to teach us that even when we think we know something inside and out, if we learn it just one more time we'll find a totally new facet that we hadn't seen before.

We have to be willing to go that extra mile if we want to harvest our fruit!

 # The Torah Reading

The Torah reading can be divided into three parts:

1. Devarim 33:1-26 is read repeatedly, until everyone in synagogue has a chance to say the blessings over the Torah.

2. Devarim 33:27-34:12. The person called up for this is called the *hatan Torah,* "groom of the Torah," because he receives the honor of completing the reading of the Torah.

3. B'raishit 1:1-2:3. The person called up for this is called the *hatan B'raishit,* "groom of B'raishit," because he receives the honor of being the first one to get called up to start the new cycle of the Torah reading.

The Maftir is the same as the one read on "Shemini Atzeret," dealing with the sacrifices of that day.

The Haftarah is taken from Yehoshua 1:1-18. After having read about Moshe's death, we now read how his disciple, Yehoshua, takes the reigns and embarks on the task of leading B'nai Yisrael into Israel.

FOR YOUR INFORMATION

1) Both at night and during the day, we do *hakafot,* "encircling." All the Torah scrolls are taken out of the Ark and we go around the *bima* seven times, while dancing and singing.

2) Everybody gets called up to the Torah to recite the blessings.

Index (by theme)

MY
D'VAR TORAH
FOR...

MY
D'VAR TORAH FOR...

MY
D'VAR TORAH FOR...

MY D'VAR TORAH FOR...

MY
D'VAR TORAH FOR...